THE MODERATELY MOTIVATED MAN'S GUIDE TO TIME MANAGEMENT

DECLUTTER YOUR DAYS AND WIN BACK YOUR TIME (WITHOUT TRYING TOO HARD)

RICK RESNICK

THE HUSBAND SCHOOL

The Husband School® presents:

*The Moderately Motivated Man's Guide to Time Management:
Declutter Your Days and Win Back Your Time
(Without Trying Too Hard)*

© 2025 Rick Resnick

The Moderately Motivated Man™ is a trademark of U.S. Explorers, LLC.

All rights reserved. No part of this book may be reproduced or transmitted in any form or by any means without prior written permission from the author, except for brief quotations in reviews. For more information, go to contact.moderatelymotivatedman.com

This book is intended for general informational and entertainment purposes only and does not constitute professional, legal, financial, or medical advice. Readers should consult appropriate professionals for guidance specific to their situation. The author and publisher disclaim any liability arising from the use of the information contained in this work.

Note on Authorship and Editorial Process:

This book was developed with the support of modern AI writing and research tools under the author's full creative direction. All final content reflects the author's voice and editorial judgment. Human editors and early readers reviewed the manuscript to ensure clarity and accuracy.

First paperback edition March 2026

First ebook edition February 2026

ISBN 979-8-9912429-2-9 (paperback)

ISBN 979-8-9912429-3-6 (ebook)

www.ModeratelyMotivatedMan.com

ALSO BY RICK RESNICK

The New Husband's Survival Guide: The Secrets to a Happy Marriage While Navigating Sex, Money and a Shared Bathroom

The Moderately Motivated Man's Guide to Habits: Start Small and Build What Lasts (Without Trying Too Hard) — Summer 2026

BEFORE WE GET STARTED

One optional thing that can make this book more useful:

DOWNLOAD THE FREE COMPANION TOOLKIT

Printable versions of the Moderately Painless Exercises and a few other handy worksheets to help you take back your time.

Scan the code below or visit:

TMtoolkit.ModeratelyMotivatedMan.com

That's it. Your call.

Now let's get into it.

ModeratelyMotivatedMan.com

CONTENTS

Preface: About This Series	7
Introduction	9
1. Embrace Time's Limits	13
2. Choose What Matters, Not What's Next	24
3. Focus Like a Human, Not a Machine	36
4. Detox from Digital Overload	48
5. Beat Procrastination	59
Intermission	69
6. Protect Your Precious Time	71
7. Build Habits That Bend, Not Break	83
8. Rest Without Regret	95
9. Become Your Best Self	105
10. Use Tools That Work	116
Conclusion	126
About the Author	129
Thank You For Reading	130

PREFACE: ABOUT THIS SERIES

WHO IS THE MODERATELY MOTIVATED MAN?

The Moderately Motivated Man is smart, capable, and self-aware. He's juggling work, home life, relationships, fitness, finances—and trying to stay on top of it all without losing his sense of humor (or his weekends).

He wants to succeed but not at the cost of missing Thursday night wings, a last-minute movie night, or lazy Sunday mornings.

He's ambitious, not obsessed. Motivated, not manic. So, yeah, he's *moderately* motivated.

He's sharp enough to know he could do better and realistic enough to know he's not about to wake up at sunrise to meditate. Or rank his life goals in a spreadsheet.

He's not looking to overhaul his life overnight, just to be a better version of himself—more focused at work, more present at home, more consistent at getting to the gym, maybe even more committed to finally learning to play that guitar gathering dust in the rec room.

PREFACE: ABOUT THIS SERIES

He's aiming for progress, not perfection. He wants to grow, not grind.

If that sounds like you, welcome to the club. Let's keep rollin'.

THE GUIDE SERIES PROMISE: SMART HELP, WITHOUT THE HYPE

The Moderately Motivated Man guide series exists for one reason: to help regular guys get better at life without turning personal development into a full-time job.

You'll find practical, real-world strategies that are simple, doable, and designed to fit your actual life—not the influencer-brandished myths on TikTok.

No yelling. No judgment. Just savvy advice, a few laughs, and zero pressure to break up with your snooze button.

Each book tackles topics men actually deal with—such as finances, fitness, and home repair—to make life easier, not more complicated.

And each book is intentionally concise—short and sweet. We're not here to waste your time with fluff or busy work. Get in. Get out. Get smarter. Move on.

Our mantra is simple: Get Better at Life *(Without Trying Too Hard)*.

This first book is on time management. Why? If you don't get a handle on that, you won't have, well, time for anything else.

INTRODUCTION

WIN BACK YOUR TIME (WITHOUT TRYING TOO HARD)

You picked up this book because you want more time—or, at least, more *control* of your time.

Your to-do list is as long as a CVS receipt. Your mornings are a blur of keys, coffee, and low-grade panic. And somehow, you got roped into organizing the guys' annual golf weekend. Again.

Your calendar is a mess. And you're tired of feeling like time owns you instead of the other way around.

If any of that sounds familiar, you're in the right place. It's time to do time management—the Moderately Motivated Man way.

You won't find 5 a.m. clubs or "just push harder, bro" here. That stuff is exhausting, and frankly, it doesn't work for most of us. Instead, this is a down-to-earth guide to making time work for you.

The book's mission is right there in the subtitle:

Declutter Your Days and Win Back Your Time. If you give us a shot, we know you can do it.

WHY TIME MANAGEMENT MATTERS

Time is the one resource you can't earn more of. You can't download it or order extra from Amazon. You've got what you've got.

So why do so many of us spend it like it's unlimited?

We drift. We scroll. We say yes to things that don't matter and no to things that do. We waste energy on work that doesn't move the needle. For the fifth week in a row, we tell ourselves we'll start something "tomorrow."

And then we wonder where the month went.

The good news? That's fixable. Not with guilt. Not with fake hustle. But a bit of clarity, a few simple tools, and some honest decisions about what matters most.

That's what you'll get here.

NO NEW THEORIES. JUST A BETTER APPROACH.

We're not reinventing time management. Many of the ideas in this book have been around for a while.

The difference is how they're delivered. We're more real than rigid. More friendly than formulaic.

We've broken down time management into 10 short, stand-alone chapters. Together, they form a flexible playbook, offering 10 clear ways to simplify your schedule and make space for what matters.

You'll learn how to do the following:

- Accept that time is limited—and why that's good news.
- Choose what matters instead of reacting to what's next.
- Focus like a human, not a machine.
- Detox from digital overload without going off the grid.
- Beat procrastination without pep talks or guilt.
- Protect your precious time by setting boundaries that stick.
- Build habits that bend instead of break.
- Rest without regret—because downtime fuels performance.
- Align your time with the man you want to become.
- Use tools that work *for* you, not *against* you.

Each chapter ends with two Moderately Painless Exercises: an "MPE Main" for deeper experiments and an "MPE Mini" for quick wins you can try in minutes. No spreadsheets or sermons—just small steps that stick.

BEFORE YOU DIVE IN

If you've read this far, give yourself credit. You're not just moderately motivated; you're *ready*. Ready to stop winging it. Ready to make your time yours.

This book won't change your life overnight, but it will give you the tools to change your relationship *with* time. You'll feel a little more in control, a little less overwhelmed, and a lot more confident that you're spending your days on what truly matters to you.

We're glad you're here. Let's get your time back.

CHAPTER 1
EMBRACE TIME'S LIMITS

CHAPTER SUMMARY

The idea that time is finite isn't meant to make you feel panicked. It's actually freeing—because once you accept that you can't do it all, you can finally stop pretending you should. You can start using time to build a life you truly enjoy living. You're not here to maximize every second; you're here to make choices that feel right. That mindset shift starts in this chapter, which gives you the big-picture context you need before diving into the practical tools in the rest of the book.

SECTION 1: THE MYTH OF "GETTING IT ALL DONE"

THE CATCH-UP ILLUSION

You've probably felt it before: that tight-chested, brain-spinning moment when you glance at your to-do list and realize there's not a chance in hell it's getting done today. Or this week. Or maybe ever.

Instead of crossing a few things off and moving on, you carry that list around like emotional luggage. You guilt yourself over the emails you didn't answer, the birthday card you forgot, and the shelf you never built. You convince yourself that if you were a little more disciplined, you'd finally "get caught up."

But caught up to what, exactly?

The myth of "getting it all done" is like chasing the horizon. It moves as you move. The harder you sprint, the more burned out you feel. This chapter is your invitation to stop sprinting and start steering.

TIME IS A NON-RENEWABLE ASSET

Remember that old saying, "Time is money"? Well forget it. Because it's wrong.

Yes, they're both resources that we spend. But here's the bottom line: You can make more money. You can't make more time.

Once an hour passes, it's gone—like that burrito you dropped in the parking lot. You can't pick it back up and try again. Spilled. Splat. Spent.

When you absorb that truth, you start thinking differently about your calendar. You stop treating it like a junk drawer for everything you "should" be doing. Instead, you ask: What's honestly worth my time?

That doesn't mean every minute has to be optimized or monetized. It means you stop giving away your best hours to things that don't matter—or worse, things that actively stress you out.

Want to feel more in control of your day? Start by treating your time as if it's priceless—because it is.

HUSTLE CULTURE IS A SCAM

If you've ever felt bad for not having a "5 a.m. routine," it's not your fault. Hustle culture sold you a dream, and it came with a side of shame.

The influencers, entrepreneurs, and productivity bros with whiteboards in their showers are all pushing the idea that success means grinding 24/7. They tell you that if you merely push a little harder, skip a few more breaks, and power through your burnout, you'll win.

Spoiler: They're selling you a treadmill. One that doesn't turn off.

Hustle culture isn't about helping you succeed. It's about keeping you busy enough to never question whether the race is worth running.

You are not a machine. You need sleep, snacks, moments of peace, time with your kids, and a shower that lasts more than 43 seconds. Productivity without purpose is only noise.

Want to win? Step off the treadmill. Redefine what "enough" means. And maybe unfollow that guy who says he built a six-figure startup during a silent meditation retreat.

YOUR TIME, YOUR VOTE

Before we dive into the how-to's, one key point: Your time isn't just hours on a clock; it's a vote for the guy you're trying to be. (We'll dig deeper into this concept in Chapter 9.)

Want to be a better dad? A sharper worker? A guy who finally fixes that squeaky cabinet door? Every choice you make with your time says something about who you're becoming.

Try this quick trick: Pick a word or two for the man you want to be this week: "Present Dad," "Healthy Guy," or "Not-Always-On-His-Phone Man." Write it down—on your phone, on a napkin, whatever. That's your North Star. As we roll through this book, you'll see how small tweaks to your time can line up with those words, without needing a life coach or a sunrise yoga obsession.

No pressure. Just a few words to steer by. Because the Moderately Motivated Man doesn't need to overhaul his life—he just needs to start voting for the right stuff.

PROGRESS BEATS PERFECTION

If you're waiting for the perfect day, the perfect energy level, or the perfect moment to start that thing you've been meaning to do ... well, you might be waiting forever.

Perfection is a moving target. It tells you you're never quite ready. That your first draft isn't good enough. That doing only five push-ups doesn't count. That organizing one drawer won't matter.

Here's the truth: Small progress compounds. A 10-minute cleanup session once a week beats an epic four-hour "get your life together" binge that never actually happens. Sending a half-decent email today beats crafting the perfect email in your head for two weeks straight.

Every little action you take today builds momentum. And momentum, not motivation, is what keeps things going.

So lower the bar. Set the bar on the floor, and step over

it with dignity because that's how progress—messy, scrappy, human progress—actually works.

SECTION 2: THE POWER OF LIMITS

DO LESS—BETTER

Now that we've buried the myth of doing everything, let's talk about what happens when you finally start doing specific things—on purpose.

Most guys think of limits as ... well, limiting. Like, if you admit you can't juggle 12 flaming swords at once, you're weak. But what if limits were your secret weapon? What if they helped you to stop juggling and start really living?

You don't need to do more. You need to do less—better.

LIMITS FORCE CLARITY

Have you ever noticed how much easier it is to decide what to do when you don't have 37 options?

If you've ever opened Netflix, stared at your queue for 12 minutes, and then given up, you already know that more options equal more paralysis.

Limits give you clarity. They help you focus. They say, "You have this much time; what's worth doing?"

This is why constraints are secretly powerful. You've got only 30 minutes? Excellent—no time for dithering. You've got two free evenings a week? Amazing—now you have to choose what truly matters to you.

Freedom doesn't come from unlimited options. It comes from making intentional choices.

DITCH THE GUILT LIST

Let's talk about The List. You know the one—the one that haunts your phone, fridge, and brain. Part chores, part dreams, part random thoughts scribbled on Post-its that you pretend you can still decipher. It's less a to-do list and more a Museum of Good Intentions.

Every time you look at it, instead of feeling inspired, you feel like a failure. "Still haven't cleaned the garage. Still haven't started that podcast. Still haven't emailed Steve back about those dumb blinds."

Here's your reality check: You're not a bad person because your to-do list is unfinished. You're a normal person living an authentic life. And that list? It's trying to guilt you into being superhuman.

So let's try something bold: Start deleting.

Not everything on your list deserves your time. Some of those tasks are long-expired invitations to projects you don't care about anymore. Some were never yours to begin with, just stuff other people thought you should do.

If it's been on your list for six months, here's a radical idea: Let it go. If it honestly mattered, you'd have done it—or at least moved it closer to the top. And if you didn't? That's data. It's your subconscious telling you, "Hey, maybe this thing doesn't belong."

You can't do everything. You can discern what's worth doing.

SECTION 3: WHO'S REALLY IN CHARGE? (HINT: YOU)

LEAD BY CHOOSING, NOT CHASING

This may sound clichéd, but here goes: You are the CEO of your life.

Now, before you grab a standing desk and order a bunch of whiteboards, hear me out. Being the CEO doesn't mean you do everything yourself. It means you decide what gets your attention, energy, and resources. That's the essence of leadership.

And leadership is not about chasing everything. It's about choosing what matters.

When you try to do everything at once, you end up reacting instead of leading. You become the assistant to your own calendar—constantly rescheduling, apologizing, scrambling, and losing track of what you actually care about.

But when you start choosing—proactively and clearly—things shift. You start saying "yes" with intention and "no" without guilt. You make time for your kid's soccer game on purpose, rather than squeezing it in around work emails. You cook dinner because you want to, not because you feel guilty about ordering takeout again.

This doesn't make you selfish. It makes you strategic. You're choosing how to spend your time, instead of letting the world spend it for you.

LIFE ISN'T A PERFORMANCE REVIEW

If you've ever ended a week thinking, "I didn't do enough," take a breath. Let's flip that script.

You're not a middle manager reporting to some invisible productivity overlord. No one is grading your ability to "crush it" every week.

In fact, most of the best stuff in life doesn't show up on a to-do list:

- Listening to your kid explain Pokémon lore for 12 straight minutes
- Rewatching a comfort movie you've seen 19 times
- Sitting on the porch doing absolutely nothing and loving it

These moments are "non-productive," but they're the ones you'll remember.

Stop measuring your life by output. Start measuring it by alignment: Were you true to your values today? Did your actions reflect what matters to you? Were you present, even for five minutes?

You don't have to *earn* rest—or get permission to feel good about your day. Life isn't a checklist; it's a story. And you get to decide what kind of story you want to tell.

DEFINE SUCCESS ON YOUR TERMS

Let's be real: A lot of us inherited our definition of success from other people—parents, teachers, bosses, Gary Vee. But when was the last time you honestly asked yourself what success looks like for you?

Here's a secret: If your idea of success stresses you out, drains your energy, or makes you feel perpetually behind, it's probably not *your* idea of success.

Success, for the Moderately Motivated Man, doesn't look like 14-hour days, inbox zero, or an overflowing calendar. It looks like alignment—where your time, energy, and attention are directed toward what matters to you.

That might be building a business. Or building LEGO sets with your kid. Or finally fixing that cabinet door that falls off every time you open it.

Success is not about volume; it's about meaning. The more you define it for yourself, the less you'll care about how anyone else defines it for you.

SMALL SHIFTS, BIG WINS

Let's close with some encouragement: This chapter is not asking you to overhaul your life.

Instead, here's what real progress looks like for the Moderately Motivated Man:

- Saying "no" to a task that doesn't matter—and feeling zero guilt about it.
- Letting something stay undone without spiraling.
- Catching yourself before you overcommit, and choosing rest instead.
- Taking 10 minutes to plan your day with intention instead of just diving in.
- Reminding yourself that "done" beats "perfect."

Small, mindful choices lead to meaningful change. One better decision today can ripple into a calmer, more intentional week.

Make sense? Great. Let's get started.

KEY TAKEAWAYS FROM CHAPTER 1

1. *The Myth of "Getting It All Done."* Time is finite, so stop acting like you have unlimited hours. The myth of catching up is a treadmill that leads to burnout, not balance.

2. *The Power of Limits.* Limits are a feature, not a flaw. When you embrace them, you reduce guilt, sharpen focus, and make better decisions—doing less, better.
3. *Who's Really in Charge? (Hint: You).* Success isn't about output; it's about alignment. Lead your time by choosing what matters, not chasing everything. Even small improvements can ripple into calmer, more satisfying days.

ACKNOWLEDGMENTS

Some clever folks helped shape the thinking in this chapter. A nod to Oliver Burkeman (*Four Thousand Weeks*) for reminding us that time is short, and that's okay. Hat tip to Talkspace for their clear-eyed take on the productivity myth. And thanks to Avi Siegel, whose Medium article, "Time Is a Finite Resource... So Create More of It (Through Better Organization)," gave us permission to organize our sock drawers and call it a life upgrade.

MODERATELY PAINLESS EXERCISES

MPE MAIN: THE BONUS TIME TEST

If a time genie offered to give you 10 extra hours next week, how would you spend them?

Seriously—pause here. Open your notes app, or grab a scrap of paper. List how you'd use that gift of time. Be honest.

Would you:

- Catch up on sleep?
- Go for a long walk without your phone?
- Call your cousin back (finally)?
- Work on your side project?
- Just sit quietly for once?

Now ask yourself: Could you sneak one of those things into your real week? If not, why not? Spoiler: The problem isn't the clock. It's the clutter.

This exercise gives you a quick window into what matters—not in some grand philosophical way, but in a "Hey, this belongs on my calendar" kind of way.

Your bonus time wish list says a lot about what matters to you—maybe more than your current calendar does.

MPE MINI: THE "NOT-TO-DO" LIST

Tonight, make a list of five things you're not going to do this week. It can be anything from "organize the garage" to "respond to emails after 6 p.m."

Don't just list things you were never going to do anyway. Make this a real trade-off.

Put the list somewhere visible. Stick to it like a champion. Sometimes the best way to make time is to stop spending it on the wrong stuff.

CHAPTER 2
CHOOSE WHAT MATTERS, NOT WHAT'S NEXT

CHAPTER SUMMARY

Successful time management is less about mastering your calendar and more about steering your life in a direction that feels right. In this chapter, the Moderately Motivated Man stops chasing productivity like a dog chasing its tail and starts making intentional, value-based decisions. We'll walk through how to identify what really matters, how to stop reacting to every ping, and how to reduce stress by making fewer, smarter choices.

SECTION 1: CHOOSE DIRECTION OVER CONTROL

CONTROL IS A MIRAGE

You know that fantasy: the mythical week when your inbox hits zero, your kid's birthday present is wrapped before the party, and you finally return that tool your neighbor loaned you ... back in 2019.

Yeah. That week doesn't exist.

The more we try to control every minute, the more life reminds us that it gets the last laugh. The dog throws up at 7:58 a.m. Meetings run late. And instead of finally organizing the garage, you're hunting down that elusive Allen wrench.

Life doesn't respond well to micromanagement. It spills, slips, forgets, delays, cancels, and glitches. And trying to schedule every breath and preload every minute doesn't make us feel more in control. It makes us feel brittle, like one push notification away from snapping.

INTENTION BEATS CONTROL

If control is a dead-end, what's the better play? Intentionality.

Now, don't worry—"intentionality" sounds like the kind of thing you'd hear in a corporate offsite or meditation retreat, but it's merely a fancy way of saying, "Do things on purpose."

When you live with purpose, you stop operating by default. You stop letting your calendar boss you around. You stop handing over your time to whoever asks for it the loudest.

Intentionality means having a plan—not only for your day, but for your *direction*. It's about choosing what matters and letting the rest take a back seat. Like a bouncer at a dive bar who knows who gets in, and who's going to be trouble.

Here's the win-win: When you *know* what matters, you get better at making decisions. No more dithering over whether to take on that extra project, attend the optional meeting, or reorganize your spice rack. When your values are clear, your schedule starts to align.

You don't need total control. You need a compass.

REACTIVE MODE IS SURVIVAL MODE

You know the feeling: You sit down in the morning with high hopes, coffee in hand, and five hours later, you've answered 46 emails, said yes to two favors you didn't really want to do, and organized your desk instead of organizing your day.

That's reactive mode. And it's exhausting.

When you live reactively, your attention becomes public property. Anyone with your email address or Slack handle gets a piece of your brain. You don't drive your day; you *respond* to it. By the time you realize what happened, the day's gone, and you didn't touch the stuff that truly mattered.

Intentional living doesn't mean ignoring people or quitting your job to go off-grid with a homemade composting toilet. It means putting *you* back in the driver's seat, being the guy who decides where your attention goes—not the one who apologizes for missing the sixth group chat message about lunch.

ENERGY IS A FINITE RESOURCE, TOO

Let's be real: Your day isn't just limited by hours. It's limited by energy.

Mental energy. Emotional bandwidth. The ability to make one more decision without throwing your phone into a lake.

Every time you choose between 12 shades of blue for

your PowerPoint or whether to answer that "quick" message from Jeff in Accounting, you're burning mental fuel. If you spend it all on low-value decisions, you won't have anything left for the good stuff—like helping your kid with homework, finishing that thing you've been meaning to write, or just sitting down and doing absolutely nothing without guilt.

The smart move isn't to "power through." It's to be stingy with your focus. Build routines. Automate decisions. Put your most important tasks in the part of the day when your brain is at full charge.

Stop spending your best brain hours answering dumb questions from strangers. Start using that energy like the finite resource it is.

SECTION 2: DECIDE WHAT MATTERS (AND WHAT DOESN'T)

DEFINE YOUR CORE VALUES

This is the part where things get real. If you don't know what matters to you, how are you supposed to spend your time wisely?

It's like going grocery shopping without a list and ending up with frozen waffles, shaving cream, and six kinds of hot sauce. Fun? Maybe. Effective? Not even close.

Your core values are your internal GPS. They tell you where to go—and what to avoid.

Your values aren't just whatever you think *sounds* good. "Family," "health," and "making a difference" are nice, but are they *yours*? Or did you pick them up because Instagram told you they're important?

Scott Jeffrey, in his work on personal core values, puts it this way: Your real values are revealed in your actions, not your slogans. They're the stuff you return to when nobody's watching. They're the common thread in your best memories, your proudest moments, and your toughest decisions.

So before you plan your time, figure out what's honestly *worth* your time.

(We'll end this chapter with a quick exercise to pin down your core values and make sure your time aligns with them.)

THE EISENHOWER MATRIX (NO MBA REQUIRED)

Let's take a moment to honor a time-tested tool that lives up to the hype: the Eisenhower Matrix.

It's simple, clever, and named after a guy who helped win World War II and run the country. So, yeah—he probably knew a thing or two about priorities.

Here's how it works: Every task belongs in one of four boxes.

- Box 1: Urgent and Important – Do it now. (deadlines, emergencies)
- Box 2: Important but Not Urgent – Schedule it. (long-term goals, relationships, health)
- Box 3: Urgent but Not Important – Delegate it. (interruptions, busywork, favors)
- Box 4: Neither – Delete it. (scrolling, over-checking email, things that don't matter)

Most of us live in Boxes 1 and 3. We're putting out fires and answering every notification like it's breaking news. It feels productive, but we're really just reacting to whatever screams the loudest.

Box 2 is where the good stuff lives. This is the quadrant for the things that matter most but rarely yell for your attention. It's where you finally write that business plan, reconnect with an old friend, book the overdue checkup, or start exercising again. These things build your future. They won't nag you today, but ignoring them always catches up.

The Eisenhower Matrix gives you a way to see your time clearly and spend it deliberately, so you don't get trapped in permanent crisis mode.

TRY A TIME AUDIT

Want a brutally honest look at your life? Track your time for a week. Not what you *think* you spend your time on —what you *actually* do.

Grab a notebook, text yourself, or doodle on whatever's handy—even those cocktail napkins at the bar. Just capture everything: the 20 minutes spent doomscrolling before bed, the 40 minutes of clicking between tabs to feel productive (without doing anything useful), and the impromptu YouTube deep-dive into home espresso machines.

When you finish, look for the leaks. Where are you burning hours without even realizing it?

Chances are you're not lazy. You're simply wasting time and energy on things that don't align with your values. Time audits help you plug the holes, so your energy goes where it belongs.

EVOLVE AS YOUR PRIORITIES CHANGE

Let's get one thing straight: Because something *used* to matter doesn't mean it still should.

Maybe five years ago, climbing the ladder was a top priority. Now? Maybe it's coaching Little League or finally having a Saturday where you don't wake up to 37 notifications from Slack.

Your values change. Your life changes. The people around you change. So yeah, your time priorities should shift, too.

Check in with yourself regularly. New job? New baby? Midlife crisis triggered by a high school reunion? All of those are excellent reasons to revisit your calendar.

There's nothing noble about clinging to an outdated to-do list. Let it go. Make space for who you are *now*, not who you were back when you thought cargo shorts were a good look.

SECTION 3: INTENTION DOESN'T MEAN INTENSITY

SKIP ENLIGHTENMENT—USE A STICKY NOTE

Some people hear "live with intention" and immediately picture themselves on a silent retreat in the mountains, drinking herbal tea, and writing haikus about their soul. Relax. That's not where we're headed.

Intentionality isn't intensity. It's not about doing everything with full-body commitment and spiritual alignment. It's about doing *something* with a little more thought than, "Well, I guess I'll recheck my email."

Living with purpose might look less like a life reboot and more like this:

- Slapping a sticky note on your monitor that says, "What matters most today?"
- Deciding not to answer emails before 10 a.m.
- Saying no to that 7 p.m. Zoom meeting with Chad from Marketing. *(Really, Chad?)*

These are small things, but they're directional. And that's the whole point. If you wait until you feel "ready" or "fully aligned" before making intentional choices, your calendar will fill itself—for everyone but you.

HABITS ARE PRE-DECISIONS

Here's a secret: The most intentional people often don't look like they're trying very hard. That's because they made smart decisions *once* and then automated them.

Think of habits as your brain's cruise control. Instead of deciding *every single day* whether to work out, answer email, or eat lunch at your desk again, you've already made that call. You've set the default.

If your morning routine includes coffee, a walk, and five minutes of planning your day, you're living intentionally before 9 a.m.—even if you're still in your gym shorts and mismatched socks.

You don't need some app that syncs with every device you own and buzzes your smartwatch every five minutes. You just need a few default systems:

- Weekly Check-In: Every Sunday night, jot down what actually matters this week. Not everything —only the big stuff.
- Recurring Calendar Blocks: Protect time for what matters. Even if that's "do nothing."

- If-Then Rules: For example, if someone asks you to join a new committee at work, wait 24 hours before answering.

These systems don't make you rigid. They help you avoid overthinking, overcommitting, and undersleeping.

KEEP IT SIMPLE

The fewer decisions you have to make, the more brain fuel you save. That's not laziness; it's efficiency.

Think Steve Jobs and his black turtlenecks—not to copy the look (unless you want to) but because it shows he didn't waste brainpower deciding what to wear every day. He had better things to do. So do you.

Defaults simplify life around your values. They clear space, cut friction, and avoid those 47 tiny decisions that steal your energy. It's not boring; it's smart living with built-in breathing room.

KEY TAKEAWAYS FROM CHAPTER 2

1. *Choose Direction Over Control.* Life's messy, and chasing control only makes you brittle. Direction gives you leverage. It keeps you steering instead of snapping every time something slips.
2. *Decide What Matters (And What Doesn't).* Your time aligns only when your values are clear. Use tools like a time audit or the Eisenhower Matrix to separate what truly matters from the noise, and be willing to cut what doesn't.

3. *Intention Doesn't Mean Intensity.* Living with purpose doesn't require a full reboot. Simple defaults, small habits, and fewer decisions protect your energy, so you can stay aligned without burning out.

ACKNOWLEDGMENTS

Thank you to Scott Jeffrey for his thoughtful framework in "7 Steps to Discover Your Personal Values," Suzanne Bates and the team at BTS for their insights in "Great Leadership Style: The Power of Intentionality," and the folks at eisenhower.me for their clear explanation in "What is the Eisenhower Matrix?" Their work helped shape this chapter's message: that living with direction—not just reaction—can make all the difference.

MODERATELY PAINLESS EXERCISES

MPE MAIN: CORE VALUES DRILL: WHAT TRULY MATTERS TO YOU?

How do you determine your core values, especially when you aren't naturally introspective? Try this useful shortcut. Grab a pen or your Notes app. This will take 10 minutes. Tops.

Step 1: *What Makes a Good Day?*

Think of a few recent occasions when you felt content or proud, even in a low-key way. What were you doing? Who were you with?

- Example 1: If it was a weekend where you got outside, saw friends, and cooked dinner, maybe you value *connection, health,* or *simplicity.*
- Example 2: You spent the afternoon working on a DIY project in the garage, lost track of time, and didn't check your phone once. Perhaps you value *focus, creativity,* or *independence.*
- Example 3: You had a day where you got everything on your list done *and* had time to relax with a movie that evening. You might value *efficiency, balance,* or *peace of mind.*

Step 2: *What Ticks You Off?*

Write down three things that regularly frustrate or annoy you—at work, at home, wherever. Now ask: What value is compromised when this happens?

- Example 1: If constant interruptions drive you crazy, maybe you value *focus* or *autonomy.*
- Example 2: You hate when people talk over you in meetings or ignore your input. You might value *respect, fairness,* or *recognition.*
- Example 3: You get irrationally irritated when plans change at the last minute. Perhaps you value *stability, reliability,* or *order.*

Step 3: *Steal From This List*

If you're stuck, circle 5–10 words from this mini-values menu that resonate with you, not ones you think you "should" pick:

Family, Growth, Creativity, Freedom, Health, Humor,

Learning, Honesty, Adventure, Service, Stability, Simplicity, Autonomy, Curiosity, Purpose, Rest.

Now look at your list and narrow it down to your top 3–5 core values. These are your guideposts. Now you have something to follow.

MPE MINI: "THE CALENDAR CLEANSE"

Block 15 minutes to look at your calendar for the next week. Find *one* meeting, commitment, or obligation that you agreed to out of habit, guilt, or autopilot, and then cancel it.

Use that reclaimed time to do something that truly matters to you: play catch with your kid, take a nap, read, or think. You've just made a proactive decision. Welcome to intentional living.

CHAPTER 3
FOCUS LIKE A HUMAN, NOT A MACHINE

CHAPTER SUMMARY

This chapter addresses one of the biggest modern myths: that multitasking is a time-saver. Guess what? It's the opposite. In reality, switching between tasks makes you less effective, more tired, and more likely to forget where your keys are (again). Here, the Moderately Motivated Man learns why focus is the real time-management weapon and how to cultivate it without needing monk-level discipline or noise-canceling everything. You'll get practical, human-friendly tools for cutting through distraction, working smarter, and actually finishing what you start.

SECTION 1: MULTITASKING IS A LIE

YOUR BRAIN CAN'T MULTITASK

Multitasking can feel productive: emailing, stirring pasta,

and replying to Slack, while half-listening to a podcast. You're like a machine, right?

Yes. And no.

Your brain isn't a computer running a dozen tabs in the background. It's not built for parallel processing. When tasks need focus or decisions, your brain works on one thing at a time.[1]

When you try to "do it all," your brain actually toggles back and forth between tasks, and every toggle costs time and mental energy.

Every time you switch tasks, there's a mental toll called *attention residue*.[2] It's the leftover focus power still clinging to the last thing you were doing, making it tougher to fully engage in the next task.

Multitasking also slows you down. Studies show that switching between tasks can cut productivity by up to 40 percent.[3] That's not just wasted time; it's a mental tax that leaves you drained without the satisfaction of real accomplishment.

This isn't a flaw. It's human. The trick is to stop fighting your brain's design and start working with it.

FOCUS IS FINITE

Think of your focus like a phone battery. Every app you open drains it. Every switch from task to task wears it down faster. And unlike your phone, your brain doesn't come with a portable charger.

When you multitask all day, you're burning through your concentration reserves faster than they can recharge. By 3 p.m., you're zoning out at the screen, wondering why typing a four-line email feels like a full-body workout.

It's actually a lose-lose: The more tasks you juggle, the

worse you get at prioritizing them. Decision fatigue sets in. You waste your best energy on nonsense, and by the time something meaningful shows up, your brain is toast.

This is why deep focus matters. It's not about intensity; it's about economy. Protect your attention as you would your time or money. Because once it's gone, it's gone.

THE FOMO TRAP

One of the most potent forces behind multitasking? Fear of Missing Out.

It's not just social media; it's the pull of every browser tab, notification, and mental ping that says, "Hey, check me right now." You might even tell yourself it's necessary: "I need to keep an eye on email ... just in case."

But every "quick check" costs you more than you think. It breaks your flow. It fractures your thinking, and it sends you down rabbit holes—like checking prices for a flight you're not actually booking or reading reviews for a toaster you don't need.

Constant scanning makes your brain skim the surface instead of sinking deep into what matters. You end up living in surface mode: busy but never anchored. It's reactive living, not intentional action.

THE COST OF DISTRACTION

If you've ever ended a day exhausted but unsure what you actually got done, you've felt the price of multitasking. You *worked* all day, but you didn't *finish* anything. You checked multiple boxes, but none of them were the big one. That's not failure; it's friction.

You're not goofing off. You're overloaded. Distracted and pulled in 14 directions.

But here's the upside: Once you stop trying to be a robot and start focusing like a human, things click. You work smarter. You finish more. And you end the day with enough gas in the tank to still be a functioning human being at home.

SECTION 2: FOCUSING ON FOCUS

TACKLE ONE TASK AT A TIME

Single-tasking means doing one thing at a time—on purpose. It sounds simple, but most of us don't actually do it. The truth is, focus doesn't require a perfect schedule or a life free from distractions. It starts by making a few intentional choices that reduce mental noise and help you finish what you start.

In this section, you'll learn a handful of simple tools to bring more focus to your day—without overhauling your personality or pretending you've got it all together. Just straightforward, usable steps that make it easier to stay on track.

LISTS FOR THE REAL WORLD

Every Moderately Motivated Man has done it: the mega list. It starts with "Email dentist" and ends with "Build patio." Somewhere in there are 28 other tasks that you optimistically think you'll knock out between meetings.

Spoiler: You won't. Write the list you actually will do—

not the one you wish you could. That slight shift changes everything.

Try this approach:

- Start with your "one big thing." If everything else falls apart, what's the one task that will make the day feel like a win?
- Batch the small stuff. Combine errands, emails, or admin tasks into one time block. Don't let them trickle across your whole day.
- Review midday. Don't wait until 5 p.m. to realize you've been doing the easy stuff all morning. Check your list after lunch. Adjust if needed.
- Use verbs. "Call," "Send," "Write," "Decide." Vague tasks, such as "Taxes," can be intimidating. Be specific: Try "Download forms" or "Email accountant."

Realistic lists keep you honest. And they let you enjoy the best feeling in the world: crossing something off.

THE POMODORO METHOD MADE SIMPLE

You may have heard of the Pomodoro Technique: Work for 25 minutes, take a 5-minute break, and repeat. It's named after one of those small tomato-shaped kitchen timers.

It's a little gimmicky, but it works. Not because timers are magic, but because your brain loves a clear finish line. It's like telling yourself, "You don't have to do this forever—just for 25 minutes." Suddenly, the task doesn't feel so overwhelming. It's no longer a mountain. It's a hill.

How to use it without hating it:

- Set a realistic goal. Choose one focused task, not "Clean out entire inbox, reorganize folders, and write a novel." Set a doable goal like "Reply to five emails."
- Use whatever timer works. Any kitchen timer will do—or if you'd rather, apps like Focus Keeper or Forest *(see Chapter 10)* can keep you honest.
- Make the break count. Don't scroll your phone. Stand up, stretch, and get water. Hell, grab a Yodel. You've earned it!
- Stack a few cycles. After 2 or 3 rounds, take a more extended break, 10 to 20 minutes. Walk around the block. Reboot your brain.

Pomodoro isn't about rigidity. It's about training your brain to sprint, not to run a marathon.

You'll get more done and feel less cooked at the end of the day.

YOUR SPACE FUELS YOUR FOCUS

Focus isn't only mental; it's environmental. Where you work, what's around you, and how your space feels all shape your ability to lock in.

You don't need a pristine office—just a spot that says, "This is where stuff gets done."

Start here:

- Pick a zone. Try one corner of the kitchen, in the car parked on a quiet street, or in the

living room chair *after* you move the laundry off it.
- Add visual cues. Try headphones, a lit candle, or your favorite mug. These things tell your brain: "We're in focus mode now."
- Reduce the noise. Close tabs. Turn off the TV. Put your phone out of arm's reach—or at least flip it face down.
- Declutter just enough. You don't need a Pinterest workspace, but a clear desk helps clear your head.

If your current environment screams "chaos," your brain will likely echo that sentiment. A few tweaks can turn almost anywhere into a decent place to work—even if it's only for 25 minutes at a time.

COMMEMORATE CROSSING THE FINISH LINE

Let's talk dopamine. Every time you finish something—check off a task, hit "send," or close that browser tab—your brain gives you a little chemical high-five. Use that.

Completion is its own reward, but you can up the stakes:

- Micro-rewards: Try a stretch break, a snack, or a guilt-free phone scroll. (Set a timer so the reward doesn't become the next rabbit hole.)
- Daily reward: Finish your top three priorities? Watch that show, or take a walk. Feel good on purpose.
- Visual tracking: Cross it off, check a box, or

move the sticky note. Seeing progress builds momentum.

Remember: You're not bribing yourself. You're reinforcing a habit—one where it feels good to complete a task, not just start it.

SECTION 3: LIVE IN THE REAL WORLD

PLAN FOR LIFE'S INTERRUPTIONS

You can't eliminate every distraction, but you can stop them from wrecking your flow. No matter how focused you are, life will inevitably poke you.

Your kid needs a snack. Your boss has "a quick ask." A neighbor wants to borrow a screwdriver (and never return it). You can't eliminate interruptions, but you can make them less disruptive.

Here's how to get proactive about the inevitable:

- Build "buffer zones." Leave 10–15 minute blocks between meetings or major tasks. Use them to reset, respond to a surprise, or merely breathe.
- Set expectations. Let your coworkers, family, or roommates know when you're in deep focus mode—and when you'll be available. A simple "I'll be free at 3:00" can stop a 2:15 interruption.
- Keep a "later list." When an idea, task, or random thought pops into your head, don't chase it; jot it down and return later. Don't try to solve everything right now.

- Create a restart ritual. When you're pulled away mid-task, have a go-to way to get back in. You can reread the last sentence, reset the timer, or start with one tiny next step.

Interruptions happen. The trick is to get better at bouncing back instead of staying off track.

REST RESTORES FOCUS

Here's something nobody tells you about focus: It's not just about discipline; it's about energy. And if you're always tired, overcommitted, or running on caffeine and fumes, no productivity hack will save you.

High performance isn't only about powering through. It's about knowing when to power down.

Recovery isn't lazy; it's strategic. Here's how to build it into your life:

- Stop pretending breaks are optional. Your brain isn't a machine; it needs rest to restore memory, creativity, and motivation. Even five minutes makes a difference.
- Wind down your day on purpose. Set a time to shut the laptop. Tidy your space. Make a quick list for tomorrow. This signals to your brain: "We're done for now."
- Protect your sleep as if it were sacred. That "one more episode" or "five more minutes of scrolling" becomes tomorrow's caffeine emergency and a brain that's not firing on all cylinders.

- Unplug your inputs. Podcasts, news, texts, and Netflix—every quiet moment gets crammed. Try real silence. You'll be surprised how many ideas start showing up again.

Deep focus isn't built in the moment. It's built in the margins. The way you rest shapes the way you work.

KEY TAKEAWAYS FROM CHAPTER 3

1. *Multitasking Is a Lie.* Your brain can't do two demanding things at once. It just toggles badly, leaving behind attention residue and draining your energy. The more you switch, the less you finish.
2. *Focusing on Focus.* Practical tools (such as realistic to-do lists and the Pomodoro method) and distraction-proof environments help you single-task, protect your attention, and actually finish what you start.
3. *Live in the Real World.* Interruptions and fatigue are inevitable. Planning for them, and prioritizing rest, keeps you from spiraling when life barges in and fuels the focus you'll need tomorrow.

ACKNOWLEDGMENTS

This chapter was informed by the research and insights of leading cognitive scientists and productivity experts, including Dr. Jennifer E. Davis's article "Multitasking and How

It Affects Your Brain Health" (BrownHealth.org), Dr. Gloria Mark's work on attention and digital distractions (University of California, Irvine), Cal Newport's *Deep Work*, and Daniel Levitin's *The Organized Mind*. Practical strategies for minimizing distractions were also inspired by "How to Create a No Distractions Work Environment" from the Sunsama team.

SOURCING:

[1] See studies by Mariano Sigman and Stanislas Dehaene (2008), Anne M. Treisman (1980), and René Marois and Jason Ivanoff (2005).

[2] See studies from Sophie Leroy (2009), Joshua S. Rubinstein, David E. Meyer and Jeffrey E. Evans (2001), and Stephen Monsell (2003).

[3] See the American Psychological Association (APA) (2006), "Multitasking: Switching Costs," with reference to Joshua S. Rubinstein et al. (2001).

MODERATELY PAINLESS EXERCISES

MPE MAIN: THE ONE-TAB CHALLENGE

Multitasking loves tabs, so let's fight back—one browser window at a time.

The next time you sit down to work on something (writing an email, shopping for a gift, or figuring out what that smell is under the sink), try this:

- Close every single browser tab.
- Reopen only one: the one you actually need for the task at hand.

- Set a 20-minute timer. Stay in the one tab until the timer dings.
- Only then should you switch or open something new.

You'll feel twitchy at first, like you're missing something. That's normal. It's the mental version of sugar withdrawal. Stick with it; it gets easier.

MPE MINI: THE DO NOT DISTURB TEST

Pick one 60-minute block this week—only one—and turn on "Do Not Disturb" across the board: your phone, laptop, and any chatty apps. No dings, no buzzes, no browser tabs whispering your name.

Set a timer. Pick a task. Go. When the hour's up, check in with yourself: Did it feel different? Better? Did your brain stretch out a little and say, "Hey, thanks"?

If it works, do it again tomorrow. You don't need a total life overhaul—just one quiet hour at a time.

CHAPTER 4
DETOX FROM DIGITAL OVERLOAD

CHAPTER SUMMARY

Modern distractions aren't only annoying; they're also designed to hijack your concentration. In this chapter, the Moderately Motivated Man confronts the constant pinging, buzzing, and scrolling that keep him from focusing on work and enjoying meaningful downtime. This isn't about living in a cabin off the grid. It's about using technology intentionally, rather than letting it use you. You'll learn how to reclaim your attention, set digital boundaries, and make peace with your devices.

SECTION 1: WHY YOUR PHONE IS A FRENEMY

YOUR PHONE IS A TERRIBLE ROOMMATE

Imagine you have a roommate who won't stop interrupting, even when you're mid-sentence. He follows you into the bathroom, chatters through dinner, and wakes you up at 2 a.m. with a fresh batch of memes. When you're talking to someone else, he clears his throat and whispers, "Hey, did you see this email?"

You'd kick him out, right?

Instead, most of us have agreed to let this dude live in our pocket because he's useful. He helps us find our keys, order tacos, track our steps, and remember birthdays. He's also the reason we feel like our attention span has gone from "page-turning novel" to "forgot what I was doing while typing this sentence."

The problem isn't your phone. It's how it has been designed and how we've been trained to respond. In this chapter, we'll unpack what all those pings, taps, and scrolls are really doing to your time. Then we'll build a more human relationship with our tech—one that actually serves your priorities instead of constantly getting in the way.

THE SCIENCE OF DIGITAL HIJACKING

Your phone doesn't just distract. It seduces.

Every buzz, ping, or badge gives you a tiny hit of dopamine, your brain's "this might be something good" chemical. It's the same trick slot machines use to keep gamblers hooked. Variable rewards—a comment, a like, or your boss saying "call me"—keep your brain addicted to checking.

The result? You start looking at your phone even when it hasn't buzzed. You feel a phantom vibration in your pocket. Simply spotting your phone (even when it's face down) can sap your brainpower during a task.[1]

(And your smartwatch is an accomplice. It's a mini

notification machine that buzzes your wrist instead of your pocket.)

Apps aren't neutral; they're designed to hijack your attention. That's the business model, and it's working really, really well.

MICRO-DISTRACTIONS ADD UP

You know that moment when you look up from your phone and realize 45 minutes have passed? All you wanted to do was check the weather, but you ended up watching a video about how flamingos sleep.

That's not a fluke.

Studies show that after an interruption—including such innocent things as a glance at an email, a "quick" Google search, or answering a text—it takes an average of 23 minutes and 15 seconds to fully return to the original task.[2]

Every little detour costs more than time; it zaps focus, invites mistakes, and leaves you mentally foggy. The scary part is that you may not even realize how fractured your attention is until you try to concentrate and come up blank.

YOUR INBOX ISN'T URGENT CARE

Let's talk about email. A lot of us treat our inbox like it's the control center of our lives. Something comes in, and we jump to respond because what if it's urgent? What if someone's waiting? What if you're the bottleneck?

Here's the thing: Most emails aren't urgent. Most don't require a response at all. And yet, we answer them compulsively, convinced we're "staying on top of things."

In reality, you're reinforcing the idea that you're always

available. As a result, everyone gets a piece of you, on demand. That's not responsiveness. That's digital servitude.

Email is a tool. It is not your boss. You're allowed to step away from it without the world falling apart.

WHEN SCREENS HACK YOUR HEAD

If you've ever felt jittery after too much scrolling or irritable after binge-watching, you're not imagining it. Digital overload hikes anxiety, disrupts emotional balance, and wrecks your sleep. The more time you spend in front of screens, the harder it becomes to sustain focus, make decisions, and wind down.

Simply having a device nearby has been shown to increase cognitive load, even if it is not actively being used. Your brain still registers its presence and continues to scan for potential activity. That means more mental clutter, more background stress, and less ability to be present in your actual life.

And when screens creep into your bedtime routine, sleep takes a hit. Blue light disrupts melatonin production, making it harder to fall asleep and easier to wake up feeling like you were hit by a small train.

Digital burnout is real. Unless you set firm boundaries, it can quietly consume your time, energy, and attention span.

SECTION 2: MAKE TECH WORK FOR YOU (NOT THE OTHER WAY AROUND)

SILENCE THE NOISE

This is the fastest, easiest win in the history of time management. Go into your phone settings and turn off notifications for anything that isn't essential.

Does your weather app really need to tell you it's cloudy? Do you need an alert every time someone posts in a group chat you considered muting three months ago? Every ding is a mental detour. Cut the noise, on both the phone *and* the smartwatch.

Keep only what truly matters—like your calendar, direct calls, and a few VIP contacts. Everything else can wait. Trust me: If it's important, it'll find you.

BATCH YOUR DIGITAL TASKS

The next time you open your email or your messages "just for a sec," ask yourself: Are you checking or are you working? Checking is a reflex. Working is intentional.

As suggested in the last chapter, batch your digital tasks into specific windows. Give yourself 20 minutes to process email, 10 minutes to check social media, or five minutes to reply to texts.

Then stop. Really.

When you do this, you reduce the mental context switching that leaves you feeling scrambled. You also retrain the people in your life to expect intentional responses, not 24/7 access.

Boundaries don't make you unresponsive. They make you effective.

DESIGNATE DIGITAL-FREE ZONES

Want to transform your brain? Start by changing your space. Pick one area of your life that becomes a no-phone zone. It could be the dinner table, the bedroom, or even the bathroom. (You know it's a thing.)

When you enter a screen-free zone, your brain knows: This is for focus, relaxation, or connection. Over time, you'll feel calmer and more present. People around you—partners, kids, friends, and coworkers—will notice in the best possible way.

PRACTICE ONE DAILY DISCONNECT

This one's deceptively simple: Unplug for 20 minutes a day. No phone, no laptop, no streaming.

Just... nothing. It might feel weird at first. Boring. Unproductive. That's kind of the point.

We've trained ourselves to fill every gap with digital noise, but boredom is where ideas come from. It's where your brain begins to stitch thoughts together, solve problems, and experience genuine emotions.

You don't need a mountain retreat. Just give your brain 20 uninterrupted minutes to breathe.

SECTION 3: REWIRE YOUR DIGITAL HABITS

UNDERSTAND THE HABIT LOOP

You don't reach for your phone every few minutes because you lack willpower. It's a habit loop: cue, routine, and reward.

- Cue: Boredom. Stress. A lull in your workday.
- Routine: Pick up your phone.

- Reward: A quick hit of dopamine—a like, ping, or headline.

This happens dozens of times a day without thinking. But here's the good news: Habit loops can be rewritten.

Start by identifying your cues. What triggers the urge to check your device? Waiting in line? Sitting in a meeting? Getting stuck on a task?

Once you spot the pattern, insert a new routine. Keep a notepad nearby. Do a one-minute stretch. Sip water. Take a breath and stare out the window like a mysterious character in a spy movie.

Anything that interrupts the automatic phone grab loosens the old loop. Even a few seconds of awareness puts you back in the driver's seat.

USE TECH TO USE LESS TECH

This may sound contradictory, but your phone can actually help you break up with ... your phone. Here are a few minimalist-friendly apps that support digital discipline:

- Forest: Grow a tree by putting your phone away.
- Freedom: Block websites and apps during focus time.
- One Sec: Add a pause before launching addictive apps, such as social media.

The goal isn't perfection; it's awareness. These apps show what's stealing your time. Once you see it, you can stop it.

SET BOUNDARIES THAT STICK

Now let's turn that vision into action. Here are some practical ways to create digital boundaries that don't feel like punishment:

- Tech-Free Times: No screens for 30 minutes after waking up and one hour before bed.
- Tech-Free Zones: Ban phones from the dinner table, bedroom, or bathroom.
- Scheduled Checks: Check email or social media 2–3 times per day, and ignore them otherwise.
- Weekend Detox: Choose one screen-free half-day each weekend. Do without emails, scrolling, or news.

Boundaries aren't restrictions. They're upgrades. You're choosing to make space for your own life, without letting algorithms, autoplay, or TikTok trends crowd it out.

DON'T QUIT—RECALIBRATE

This isn't about demonizing technology. Don't throw your phone in a lake or buy a flip phone from 2006. You just need to recalibrate the relationship.

When you're intentional with your tech, you start using it *for* you, instead of letting it *use* you.

- You send messages instead of doomscrolling.
- You watch one show instead of 10 clips.
- You read a book instead of cycling through five apps in five minutes.

This isn't about digital perfection—just fewer distractions and more intention.

KEY TAKEAWAYS FROM CHAPTER 4

1. *Why Your Phone Is a Frenemy.* Your devices aren't neutral tools; they're designed to hijack your attention. Every ping and scroll chips away at your focus, energy, and even sleep.
2. *Make Tech Work for You (Not the Other Way Around).* Turn off nonessential notifications, batch your digital tasks, and set screen-free zones or times. Simple boundaries help you reclaim control without quitting technology.
3. *Rewire Your Digital Habits.* Checking your phone is a habit loop, not a character flaw. By spotting your cues and swapping in better routines, or even using apps that limit other apps, you can reset your relationship with tech, one tap at a time.

ACKNOWLEDGMENTS

This chapter was informed by insights from experts on digital well-being and attention management, including Lisa Keer's article "Digital Distraction and Its Impact on Your Health" (Mass General Brigham), the ThedaCare article "How to Set Technology Boundaries," and Sim Local's guide "Digital Detox: How to Reduce Screen Time Without Losing Your Mind." Foundational research on multitasking and digital overload was also supported by the American Psychological Association's report "Multitasking: Switching Costs."

SOURCING:

[1] Adrian F. Ward, Kristen Duke, Ayelet Gneezy and Maarten W. Bos (2017), "Brain Drain: The Mere Presence of One's Own Smartphone Reduces Available Cognitive Capacity."

[2] Gloria Mark, Daniela Gudith, & Ulrich Klocke (2008), "The Cost of Interrupted Work: More Speed and Stress." (Specific time of 23:15 cited by Mark in a 2008 interview with *Fast Company*.)

MODERATELY PAINLESS EXERCISES

MPE MAIN: WRITE YOUR TECH VISION STATEMENT

It's easy to say, "I should use my phone less." It's harder to say why or how—and that's where this exercise comes in. Take 10 minutes (yes, just 10) and write a short "Tech Vision Statement" for yourself. A few sentences, max.

Here's what to include:

- What you want tech to do for you (stay in touch with friends, simplify errands, or help you learn)
- What you want to avoid (mindless scrolling, interrupted sleep, or strained relationships)
- How you want to feel when you're using it—and when you're not

Your goal isn't to create a perfect plan. It's to start being intentional.

Stick it in your notes app. Scribble it on an index card. Put it somewhere you'll trip over it later. Future-you will be glad you did.

Here's a sample tech vision statement. Steal it if you'd like. Better yet, swap in the things you care about and make it your own:

"I want technology to help me stay connected to the people I care about, handle my work efficiently, and give me access to things that genuinely enrich my life—like maps, music, and reminders to take out the trash.

"I don't want it to steal hours from my day, interrupt dinner, or make me feel like I'm always 'on.' I want to be present when it counts—at the dinner table, during conversations, and when I'm winding down at night.

"I'll use my devices on purpose, not out of habit. And I'll remind myself that 'off' is a perfectly valid setting."

MPE MINI: NOTIFICATION-FREE COFFEE

Tomorrow morning, drink your coffee (or tea) without touching your phone—no alerts, apps, or screens. And ... sit there.

Notice what thoughts pop up. What urges hit. What your hands do when they're not scrolling.

You're not just detoxing your device; you're reacquainting yourself with stillness.

CHAPTER 5
BEAT PROCRASTINATION

CHAPTER SUMMARY

Procrastination isn't laziness. It's your brain's attempt to avoid discomfort, perfectionism, or decision overload by doing literally anything else. In this chapter, we'll dismantle the myth of "waiting for the right time" and replace it with something better: smart momentum. You'll learn how to break down big tasks into smaller pieces, lower the bar to get started, and reframe your resistance so it doesn't take over. The "perfect time" isn't coming, but that's okay. You don't need it.

SECTION 1: THE REAL REASON YOU PROCRASTINATE

YOU'RE NOT LAZY— YOU'RE DODGING DISCOMFORT

Let's cut to the chase: Most procrastination isn't about

discipline. You're not stalling because you lack motivation. You're dodging discomfort.

That task you keep avoiding? It probably stirs up confusion, frustration, or a fear of failure. Psychologists call this "task aversion." It's like your brain flashing a giant neon sign that screams "NOPE" the second you consider starting.

But here's the double-whammy: Not doing the task doesn't make the discomfort go away. In fact, it usually piles on a second feeling: shame. "Why didn't I start this earlier?" "What's wrong with me?" Cue the shame spiral. Now your brain is juggling dread *and* guilt, which makes the task feel even worse.

This is where many Moderately Motivated Men get stuck: trapped in the emotional quicksand of self-judgment, waiting for motivation to magically show up. (Narrator: It doesn't just magically show up.)

Here's what works instead: Drop the guilt. Accept that the discomfort is a natural part of the process. Then shrink the task to something so easy your brain can't panic. You're not waiting to feel like doing it. You're just starting—imperfectly, awkwardly, but moving forward.

CUT BIG JOBS DOWN TO SIZE

Here's a mental trick your brain loves: taking a medium-sized job and blowing it up into a towering behemoth. You say "clean the garage," and suddenly you're envisioning a 12-hour expedition involving a headlamp, a back brace, and a tetanus shot.

No wonder you've decided instead to tweak your fantasy lineup—for next season.

What's the solution? Shrink the scope. Instead of "clean the garage," try "open the garage door and throw out one empty box." That's it. That's the win. Because once you start, momentum kicks in. Action begets action.

Vague tasks are especially problematic. "Do taxes" is a motivational black hole. "Download W-2" is doable. When you make the task concrete, your brain stops panicking and starts cooperating.

If you're a digital guy, apps like Todoist or Trello *(see Chapter 10)* let you create those tiny, specific tasks so you're never staring at a foggy "plan vacation" again.

PERFECTIONISM: PROCRASTINATION IN A FANCY SUIT

There's a version of procrastination that wears a fancy suit and talks about "standards." It's called perfectionism. It tells you that if you're not going to do it right, you shouldn't do it at all.

Sounds noble. But really, it's actually anxiety with a clipboard.

Perfectionism whispers: The conditions aren't right, the plan's not ready, or you need more time, more research, or better pens. So you wait. And fidget. And stall. And nothing gets done.

This is a trap. Perfectionism isn't about excellence; it's about fear. Fear of getting it wrong. Fear of looking stupid. Fear that whatever you produce will expose you as not quite smart enough, talented enough, or put-together enough. So instead of risking flawed action, you opt for flawless inaction.

What breaks the trap? Permission to be lousy. To start scrappy. To take one step, even if it's crooked. Progress starts not with brilliance but with motion.

The moment you give yourself permission to be mediocre (at least at the start), you unlock momentum. You stop aiming for a masterpiece and start building a path.

Here are some practical ways to break the perfectionism loop:

- Use a timer to limit your "getting ready" phase. Give yourself 10 minutes to outline, and then move.
- Set deliberately low expectations for the first round. Tell yourself, "This is the rough draft *on purpose.*"
- Decide in advance what "good enough" looks like. If you wait to feel it, you'll keep moving the goalposts.
- Talk back to the perfectionist voice in your head. When it says, "This isn't quite right," respond with, "It doesn't have to be. Not yet."

Progress doesn't come from having the best plan; it comes from being willing to take the first step. Action is what separates the endlessly tweaking from the quietly achieving.

Start rough. Polish later. You can't edit a blank page.

SECTION 2: ACTION SPARKS MOTIVATION

LOWER THE BAR TO GET MOVING

Here's the hard truth for the Moderately Motivated Man: If you're waiting for motivation to show up like a Hollywood coach yelling "You can do this!"—you're gonna be waiting a long time.

Motivation is flaky. It ghosts you the moment things get tough and shows up only after you've already started. That's not a personal flaw. It's how the brain works.

The smarter move? Don't wait for a spark; just take the tiniest step forward. Something so small it feels almost laughable. Like writing the subject line of the email. Putting one dish in the dishwasher. Opening the doc. These little actions create momentum. They bypass the internal debate and get you moving.

Forget the overthinking. Ease into it. Start before you feel ready, and keep the bar low on purpose. Once you're in motion, your brain gets on board. Dopamine starts flowing. Now motivation is chasing you instead of the other way around.

CELEBRATE SMALL WINS

Let's talk about rewards. Not the gold star kind. The science-backed kind.

Every time you complete a task—even a small one—your brain gives you a shot of dopamine. That's the neurochemical version of a high-five. It reinforces the behavior, making it more likely you'll do it again.

So, don't wait until the entire project is complete. Celebrate small wins.

Replied to that email? Take a walk. Sent the invoice? Grab a snack. Got through a phone call you were dreading? Fire up a five-minute Spotify break.

The point isn't to bribe yourself; it's to make progress feel good. That's because it *is* good. Your brain already knows this. You just have to let yourself feel it.

SECTION 3: REMOVE THE FIRST HURDLE

DON'T LET SMALL STUFF STALL YOU

Here's a sneaky truth about procrastination: It's often powered by something *dumb*. You don't start the task for seemingly silly reasons such as:

- The file is lost.
- Your login is forgotten.
- Your favorite pen is AWOL.

These little roadblocks seem minor but add up fast. Soon, your brain links the whole task with friction, so you avoid it.

Here's one of the smartest anti-procrastination moves you can make: Remove the first hurdle. Make the first step so easy and obvious that it requires no mental effort to begin.

Planning to write tomorrow morning? Pop open the doc tonight. Drop in a title. Let that cursor blink like a tiny beacon calling you back. Want to do your taxes this weekend? Put the folder on your desk and write a sticky note that says "Open Me."

These aren't hacks. They're breadcrumbs, little cues that guide your future self back to the trail without hesitation.

DITCH DISTRACTIONS BEFORE THEY DISTRACT

Here's a part we often overlook: Even if you create the

perfect setup, distraction is always waiting in the wings. So before you begin, shut down the temptations.

We've talked about some of this stuff already in earlier chapters. Close unnecessary tabs. Silence notifications. Turn off Slack, email, or any other app that keeps whispering, "Check me, just for a second." That smartwatch buzzing on your wrist? Mute it.

You're not trying to resist distraction all day. You're trying *not to invite it in the first place.*

Procrastination thrives in cluttered environments—mental, digital, or physical. Simplify the space, and you simplify the start.

SPECIFIC TASKS GET DONE

Let's play a game. Which task are you more likely to do?

- "Do taxes" **X**
- "Download W-2 and check for 1099s" ✓
- "Organize kitchen" **X**
- "Clear out expired stuff from the top shelf" ✓
- "Work on proposal" **X**
- "Draft three bullet points under section one" ✓

When tasks feel vague, your brain treats them like a foggy, scary path. When they're specific and actionable, your brain sees a way in. You've reduced the emotional weight.

This isn't semantics. It's a strategy. The more concrete your action, the more cooperative your brain becomes. It's like giving yourself a mental starting line instead of a maze.

SHRINK THE TASK EMOTIONALLY

Even when a task is technically small, it can *feel* enormous. That's emotional weight, and it's sneaky.

Don't try to finish the whole project. Only the next 15-minute slice.

Here's a neat trick: Imagine the task is for someone else—your kid, your best friend, your neighbor. Would you expect them to finish the whole thing in one go? Or would you say, "Just do the next piece, then take a break"? Now say that to yourself.

Use checklists, timers, or visual milestones to help you stay on track. Break the blob into bricks. Show yourself that it's not a mountain; it's a staircase. You only have to climb one step at a time.

KEY TAKEAWAYS FROM CHAPTER 5

1. *The Real Reason You Procrastinate.* Procrastination isn't laziness; it's emotional friction. You're avoiding discomfort, perfectionism, or vague tasks, not failing at discipline.
2. *Action Sparks Motivation.* Motivation rarely comes first. Small, scrappy actions generate momentum, and momentum pulls motivation in behind it.
3. *Remove the First Hurdle.* Tiny obstacles stall progress. Break tasks into concrete steps, and clear away friction so starting feels easy and automatic.

ACKNOWLEDGMENTS

This chapter draws on key insights from several excellent sources, including the following: Dr. Itamar Shatz's "Why People Procrastinate" (SolvingProcrastination.com) unpacked the emotional roots of delay, while Ahona Guha's Psychology Today article "Instead of Waiting for Motivation, Build Habits" offered practical strategies for getting started without waiting for inspiration. And Dr. Rebecca AE Smith's "The Perfect Trap" sheds light on how perfectionism can quietly sabotage decision-making and momentum.

MODERATELY PAINLESS EXERCISES

MPE MAIN: THE FIVE-MINUTE PUSH

Let's be honest: Most of the time, the hardest part isn't *doing* the thing; it's *starting* the thing. So let's hack that hesitation. Here's your challenge:

Pick one thing you've been putting off. It doesn't matter what it is—something small (laundry), medium (responding to that email), or looming (taxes).

Set a timer for five minutes. Start the task. Don't set a goal to finish or "get in the zone." Just start. Five minutes only.

What usually happens?

- You build a little momentum.
- You surprise yourself by continuing.
- Or you stop after five. That's okay because five is still more than zero.

Remember: You're not trying to win the productivity Olympics. You're simply nudging yourself forward—one short burst at a time.

Bonus: Keep a sticky note or journal nearby. Every time you use the 5-minute trick, make a quick note of what you did. (And perhaps what the next step is.) You'll start to see how often "just a little" turns into "actually got something done."

Start small. Stay scrappy. Five minutes at a time.

MPE MINI: THE "START UGLY" SPRINT

Pick one task you've been avoiding—not because it's hard, but because it's annoying, vague, or "not quite ready yet."

Now do one imperfect version of it. Start it ugly.

Write the messy first paragraph. Open the doc and slap a title on it. Pull one drawer out instead of "organizing the whole office." Make a move, even if it's clunky.

Perfection can wait. Today is about motion. You're not finishing it. You're just breaking the seal.

INTERMISSION

A WELL-DESERVED BREAK FOR THE MODERATELY MOTIVATED MAN

If you're reading this, you've made it through the first half of the book, which means you're already ahead of 90 percent of people who start self-help books. (We have no actual data to back that up, but it feels true, doesn't it?)

This isn't a checkpoint. There are no goals, hacks, or exercises here. Just a well-earned breather.

WELCOME TO THE *HALFTIME LOUNGE*

The lights are dim. The chairs are oversized and surprisingly supportive. A small plate of something crunchy awaits. The drinks? Ice cold.

No networking. No new skills. No optimization. Just sitting.

This is your halftime. It's a well-deserved break. Just a small moment of... *ahhh*.

Close your eyes for a few seconds. Or don't. No pressure.

Flip the page now. Or in five minutes. We'll wait. The book isn't going anywhere.

When you're ready to continue, we'll be here with more friendly words, low-pressure tools, and the same calm assurance that you're doing fine.

And if anyone asks what you're doing, you can say: "I'm in the lounge. I'll be out when I'm good and ready."

CHAPTER 6
PROTECT YOUR PRECIOUS TIME

CHAPTER SUMMARY

You can't do everything, but the world will keep asking anyway. This chapter shows the Moderately Motivated Man how to protect his precious time by learning to prioritize what matters, say no with confidence, and delegate without guilt. It's not about being selfish. It's about being smart. Because if you don't control your schedule, someone else will—guaranteed.

SECTION 1: SAY NO WITHOUT GUILT

THE POWER OF NO

Let's start with the word most of us avoid at all costs: "No."

We've been trained—consciously or not—to think that saying no makes us the bad guy. If we don't jump in, show up, or stay late, we're letting people down. But because time is finite, the tradeoff is unavoidable: Every time you say yes to something that doesn't matter, you're saying no to something that does.

And let's be honest: Your schedule's jam-packed. What you need isn't more commitments, but fewer regrets.

Saying no isn't rude. It's responsible. And in many cases, it's the most respectful thing you can do—for yourself and others.

"NO" IS A FULL SENTENCE

High performers know this: Focus is power. It's less about doing more, and more about doing what truly matters. And doing what matters means safeguarding your time the same way you manage your money or health.

You don't have to justify every "no" with a five-point apology and a flow chart. A simple, polite "I can't take that on right now" is not only acceptable; it's admirable.

Why? Because people who prioritize are people who get things done.

You've seen it: The most competent guy in the room becomes the go-to. But unless he sets boundaries, he ends up constantly behind, burned out, and wondering why he agreed to coach the office softball team.

Don't be that guy.

MASTER THE "SOFT NO" AND THE "HARD NO"

Let's make this practical. A "soft no" is a gentle way to decline without slamming the door. Examples:

- "Thanks so much for thinking of me. My plate's full right now."

- "That sounds great, but I'm stretched pretty thin this week."
- "I'd love to, but I've committed to keeping things lighter this month."

Sometimes a soft no won't cut it. That's where the "hard no" comes in. Examples:

- "I'm not available for that."
- "I've decided not to take on any new projects."
- "No, I won't be able to help with that."

It feels blunt, but clarity is kindness. You're not ghosting people; you're being honest—without waffling, hedging, or offering false hope.

Having go-to phrases in your back pocket lowers the stress of the moment. No scrambling. No explaining. You're simply hitting "send" on a sentence that protects your priorities.

EXPECT PUSHBACK—AND STAY CALM

Not everyone's going to cheer when you start drawing lines in the sand. Some people will push. Some will pout. A few will try to guilt-trip you into backing down. That's okay. It doesn't mean you did anything wrong. It just means your "no" is new to them.

Their discomfort isn't your emergency.

They may not be accustomed to you having boundaries. That's not a reason to abandon them. In fact, the longer you've been the "yes man," the more important it is to shift the pattern.

Stay kind. Stay calm. Don't flinch. Don't argue or over-explain. Confidently hold your line. Most people will respect it, especially when you deliver it with respect.

TRADE GUILT FOR CLARITY

Let's talk about guilt, that weird, heavy feeling that creeps in after you say no, even when you know it was the right move.

Here's the deal: Guilt isn't proof that you did something wrong. It's just your brain reacting to a new behavior. One that prioritizes your time, energy, and sanity.

Instead of feeling guilty for protecting your time, try feeling clear. Clear about your values. Clear about your commitments. Clear about what's actually sustainable for you.

Say no clearly. Say it kindly. Then stop explaining. You don't owe anyone a backstory. You owe it to yourself to have a life that works.

SECTION 2: SHARE THE LOAD

DELEGATE LIKE A GROWN-UP

Let's start with a radical idea: Doing everything yourself doesn't make you noble. It makes you exhausted.

There's no badge of honor for being the guy who loads the dishwasher while rage-muttering because no one else "does it right." Or for staying up late to finish a report when someone on your team could've knocked it out by Tuesday.

Delegation isn't giving up. It's growing up. It's knowing your limits, protecting your energy, and trusting others to do their part—even if it's not done your way, on your timeline, or with quite the same flair you'd use when folding towels.

AVOID THE "ONLY I CAN DO THIS" TRAP

You know that voice in your head? The one that says, "I'd rather just do it myself"? Yeah, that voice is a classic control freak. Sure, you *can* do it yourself. But that doesn't mean you *should*.

Here's a better question: What are the things only you can do? Your time is finite, remember? Spending it on things that someone else could handle (even imperfectly) is a great way to burn yourself out and slow everyone else down.

Try this: List three things you're handling now that could be shared, swapped, or skipped. Laundry. Grocery runs. Chasing down RSVPs for your kid's birthday party. Are you the best person for all of those jobs? Or just the most available?

Delegating doesn't make you less valuable. It frees you to bring your best self where it counts most. Like showing up fully present. Or simply staying awake past 8:30 p.m., instead of nodding off in your work clothes.

START AT HOME: SHARE THE CHORES

This isn't about assigning chores like you're the foreman of a reluctant crew. It's about acting like partners.

If you live with someone—spouse, kids, roommates, or co-conspirators—it's time to talk about roles. Not in a finger-pointing "you never take out the trash" kind of way, but in a "how do we want our lives to run?" sort of way.

Don't tackle everything at once. Just ask: "What's

something we could shift this week so I'm not underwater?"

Maybe it's trading chores. Perhaps it's taking turns making school lunches. Maybe it's letting go of perfection and deciding that "good enough" counts as a win.

Your family doesn't need a martyr. They need you—rested, reasonable, and not secretly resenting the laundry pile.

DELEGATE AT WORK WITH CONFIDENCE

We're not writing a corporate leadership book here, but let's be honest. Most Moderately Motivated Men wear at least two hats: human and worker.

Workplace delegation counts, and yes, it's okay to ask for help. Start with clarity:

- What needs doing?
- Who's best suited?
- What's the outcome?
- When does it need to happen?

When you frame delegation as an opportunity, not a chore, it lands better. "Would you be open to leading this? It's a great stretch assignment," works a lot better than, "I can't deal with this. Can you?"

Remember: Delegation doesn't mean walking away. Set people up to succeed. Encourage questions. Don't disappear. But do resist the urge to hover like a worried parent at a science fair. That's not delegating; that's smothering in a business-casual disguise.

OUTSOURCE WHAT YOU HATE

Not everyone has the budget to hire a cleaning service or a landscaper. But if something drains your soul and there's a way to pay someone else to do it, consider it.

Outsourcing isn't cheating. It's choosing. You can't pay someone to parent your kid, but you can pay someone to mow your lawn and open up some together time on the weekend.

If Instacart saves you 90 minutes and three impulse buys, use it. If a neighborhood kid can walk the dog a couple of times a week, that's one less tug-of-war at dinnertime.

This isn't about luxury. It's about energy, time, and sanity. If you can afford to trade a little money for a lot of peace, do it.

Here's the truth: You don't get extra life points for doing it all yourself; you just get more stress.

SECTION 3: SET BOUNDARIES THAT STICK

OWN YOUR TIME—WITHOUT APOLOGIZING

Setting boundaries sounds easy enough. In practice, it often feels like standing in front of a steamroller with a hand-painted STOP sign.

But boundaries are how you protect the life you're trying to build. Without them, other people's priorities become your to-do list. Fast.

Let's talk about four ways to make those boundaries real and durable enough to last longer than a motivational podcast.

1. Define What's Non-Negotiable

If you don't know what your boundaries are, how can anyone else?

Start by identifying your "non-negotiables." These are the things that matter most: the activities, people, or blocks of time that deserve your complete protection.

Maybe it's dinner with your family. Or your morning run. Or not checking email after 8 p.m.

Name them. Write them down with a Sharpie, not a pencil. Then, when someone asks you to flex? You won't flinch. You'll already know where you stand.

2. Lead With Values, Not Excuses

There's no need to launch every "no" with a paragraph of reasons. You can lead with your values instead.

Let's say someone asks you to take on a side project, and you're already maxed out. Try this:

"I appreciate the offer. It means a lot. But right now, I'm focused on keeping my commitments tight, so I can give my full attention to what I've already said yes to."

That's not a dodge. It's values in action: commitment, focus, and integrity.

You're not saying, "I can't because I'm busy." You're saying, "I won't because I'm focused."

One feels like a dead end. The other feels like direction.

3. Get Comfortable with Discomfort

Here's the part nobody talks about: Boundaries are awkward at first.

There will be silence after you say no. There will be visible disappointment. You may sweat.

Hold the line anyway.

You're not doing anything wrong. You're just not doing what someone else wanted. Guess what? The world won't end. In fact, it will probably respect you more for it.

The more you practice, the more your nervous system catches up. That tension in your chest? It gets lighter. That fear of judgment? It fades.

Boundaries aren't walls. They're fences with gates that you control. You get to decide what's inside. You also get to lock the gate when needed, without apologizing for having a fence at all.

4. Start Small, Then Stay Consistent

Don't start by saying no to your boss or canceling Thanksgiving with your in-laws.

Begin with low-stakes boundaries. Say no to the group chat. Turn off notifications after 9 p.m. Tell a friend, "I'd love to hang out, but I'm taking tonight to recharge."

Every small act reinforces your right to protect your time and energy. And when you do say yes, say it on purpose. Say it because it fits. Say it because you honestly want to—not because you were afraid to say no.

That's the power of boundary-setting: It gives your "yes" its value back.

Remember: You don't need more hours in the day. You need fewer thieves stealing the hours you've got. Say no with purpose. Share the load. Hold the line.

KEY TAKEAWAYS FROM CHAPTER 6

1. *Say No Without Guilt.* Every "yes" has a cost. When you agree to something you don't really want to do, you're also saying no to something that truly matters. Protect your time by saying no clearly and kindly—without guilt, apologies, or long explanations.
2. *Share the Load.* Doing everything yourself isn't noble; it's exhausting. Delegation is how you protect your energy and let others step up. At home or at work, share the load so your time and attention go where they matter most.
3. *Set Boundaries That Stick.* Boundaries don't build themselves. Define your non-negotiables, hold the line with confidence, and give real value back to your "yes."

ACKNOWLEDGMENTS

This chapter draws on insights from Dr. Michelle Rozen's "How to Say No Effectively Without Guilt or Conflict," Kwame Christian's "Setting Boundaries: How to Say No with Confidence" on Forbes.com, and Michael Feder's article "5 Tips for Delegating Tasks Effectively" for the University of Phoenix. Their contributions to practical self-leadership and boundary-setting helped shape the tools shared in these pages.

MODERATELY PAINLESS EXERCISES

MPE MAIN: YOUR DELEGATION DRAFT BOARD

Goal: Identify everyday tasks you could delegate—at home, at work, and even in your social life—so you're not doing everything by default.

Step 1: *Pick Three Zones*

Create three simple headings: Home, Work, Play / Personal Life

Step 2: *Under Each Zone, List 2–3 Things You Currently Handle Yourself*

No overthinking. Jot down stuff you're doing now. Examples:

- Home: Making every school lunch. Mowing the lawn. Managing the bills.
- Work: Formatting reports. Organizing meetings. Following up on emails someone else could send.
- Play / Personal Life: Booking all the group trips. Running the fantasy league. Being the snack guy at every pickup game.

Step 3: *Ask the Magic Question*

For each task, answer: "Am I the only person who can do this?" If not, congrats. You've found a delegation opportunity.

Maybe it's time to rotate lunch duty with your partner. Perhaps you can let a teammate take over meeting prep. You can say, "I'm happy to join the trip, but someone else needs to book the Airbnbs this time."

Step 4: *Delegate One Task This Week*

Choose one task to delegate, trade, or outsource this week. Try it out. See how it feels. It might just feel fantastic!

Why It Works: When you name it, you can change it. Delegation doesn't start with confrontation; it begins with awareness. Once you identify where your energy is leaking, you can start patching the holes.

MPE MINI: DEFINE ONE NON-NEGOTIABLE

What's one thing you want to protect this week?

Family dinner? A workout? A half-hour of silence after work?

Name it. Block it off. Treat it like a meeting you can't miss. So you won't.

CHAPTER 7
BUILD HABITS THAT BEND, NOT BREAK

CHAPTER SUMMARY

Forget perfect discipline. You need systems that can withstand bad days. This chapter shows the Moderately Motivated Man how to create realistic, flexible habits that stick. Rigid routines fall apart the moment life throws a curveball (and life always throws curveballs). The real key to consistency? Start small, adapt often, and give yourself room to recover.

SECTION 1: WHY FLEXIBLE ROUTINES WIN

RIGID ROUTINES BREAK

Let's be clear: You are not a robot. You are a human—with family, meetings, neck cramps, flat tires, and late-night YouTube spirals to recover from. Then why do so many time management gurus expect you to operate like a finely tuned machine?

The problem with rigid routines is that they break. All it takes is one sick kid, one 7 a.m. dentist appointment, or one email from your boss labeled "urgent"—and suddenly, your neatly planned morning routine is toast.

The danger is that when one step breaks, the whole chain falls apart. Maybe you were going to get up early, do a workout, review your goals, and then make a smoothie with kale. (That's what disciplined people are supposed to do, right?)

What happens if you sleep for an extra 15 minutes? Now you're annoyed, skipping the workout, grabbing a gas station muffin, and wondering why you even try.

Flexible systems, on the other hand, bend. They adapt. They give you room to pivot and still feel like you're on track. Flexibility doesn't mean chaos; it's resilience.

As Harvard researcher John Beshears discovered, rigid expectations don't make routines more likely to stick in the long term. In fact, they're more likely to backfire. In his study of thousands of Google employees, those who had a strict "work out at this time every day" regimen were less likely to maintain their exercise routine than those with a more flexible approach.

Life is unpredictable. If your routine can't handle surprises, it's not sustainable. And if it's not sustainable, it's not working.

START WITH ANCHOR HABITS

Before we talk about building new habits, let's start with the ones you already have—whether you realize it or not.

Anchor habits are the simple, automatic things you do almost every day, without much thought. Brushing your teeth. Pouring your morning coffee. Starting the car. Opening your laptop. Checking your email.

These are your built-in routines, your reliable footholds in a day that might otherwise feel unpredictable.

They're not aspirational. They're already happening. And that's what makes them so valuable.

Why? Because they give you a stable platform to build on. These actions are so baked into your day that they become perfect anchor points for stacking something new. If you want a habit to stick, attach it to one you never forget.

We'll get to how that works in a minute. For now, just take stock:

- What are the things you already do on autopilot?
- Which ones show up early in the day or at predictable times?

That's your starting line—not some idealized morning routine with green smoothies and sunrise yoga. Just you, your real life, and the things you already do.

HABIT STACKING, SIMPLIFIED

Now that you've identified a few anchor habits—those daily actions you already do without thinking—it's time to build on them.

Enter: habit stacking.

Popularized by James Clear and grounded in BJ Fogg's *Tiny Habits*, the idea is simple: Pair a new habit with something you already do. You're not inventing time; you're just hitching a ride. Examples:

- After I pour my morning coffee, I do one set of push-ups.
- After I brush my teeth, I review tomorrow's calendar.
- After I open my laptop, I take 60 seconds to breathe and set my intention.

The beauty is that your anchor habits act as natural prompts. They're already wired into your routine. You're not trying to force something new into a packed schedule; you're letting it piggyback on what's already happening.

Yes, it sounds small. That's the point. Small equals repeatable. Repeatable equals powerful.

This isn't about ambition. It's about reducing friction. Less mental effort means a greater chance the habit will stick.

PERMISSION TO PIVOT

Let's be honest: Some of us were trained to believe that changing a routine means failing. We think that if we pivot, we're "giving up" or "cheating."

Nope. Not even close. Changing routines means you're adjusting to reality. It means you're paying attention. It means you're being a grown-up.

Let's say you planned to run every morning, but after a week, you realize you hate mornings … and running. You're not failing; you're learning. Try stretching at lunch or walking after dinner. The best system is the one that works *for you.*

There's no award for sticking to a broken plan. Real success comes from designing systems that adapt to your life, not fight against it.

Give yourself permission to pivot. That's not quitting. That's adapting. And that's what keeps habits alive.

SECTION 2: STICK WITH IT (EVEN ON BAD DAYS)

THE TWO-MINUTE HABIT RULE

Here's the most useful trick no one taught us in school: If you want to start a new habit, make it laughably easy—like, two minutes easy.

Want to start meditating? Sit down and close your eyes for two minutes. Want to stretch more? Touch your toes once. Want to journal daily? Write one sentence.

Fogg calls this "Tiny Habits." Clear calls it the "Two-Minute Rule." Call it what you like, but just do it.

Why does this work? Because it removes the biggest obstacle: getting started.

The brain loves inertia. If you're doing nothing, it wants to keep doing nothing. But if you're already in motion—even for two minutes—it's much easier to keep going. Those two minutes might turn into ten. Or not. That's okay. The point isn't performance. It's consistency.

Consistency builds trust in yourself. It shapes the identity you want—one tiny win at a time.

Start small. Stay consistent. Let momentum do the heavy lifting.

TRACK PROGRESS, NOT PERFECTION

You don't need a bullet journal, a spreadsheet, or a smart ring. You just need a way to see that you're showing up.

A calendar with big red Xs. A sticky note on the fridge. If you'd rather keep things digital, lightweight habit-tracking apps can do the same job *(see Chapter 10)*. Try anything that helps you visualize consistency.

Remember, your goal isn't to be perfect. Your goal is to build a trendline. Miss a day? No big deal. Just don't miss two in a row. As Clear says, the key isn't avoiding failure. It's getting back on track fast.

That visual cue—a row of Xs or a string of checkmarks—tells your brain: "This matters. Keep going." It's the difference between letting habits drift away and deciding to stick with them.

VISUAL CUES BEAT WILLPOWER

Willpower is great until it's not. And for most of us, it's not.

By 4 p.m., your willpower has been drained by emails, toddlers, coworkers, traffic, and that random text from your bank that made your stomach drop.

Don't rely on willpower. Rely on design. Set up visual cues that remind you what you wanted to do:

- A Post-it note on the bathroom mirror: "Stretch = Less back pain."
- A reminder app that buzzes at 9:30 p.m.: "Phone down. Bed wins."
- A water bottle placed on your keyboard at night, so it's the first thing you grab in the morning.

Design beats discipline. Shape your environment to steer you toward action. It's not cheating. It's smart.

REBOOT WITHOUT DRAMA

You *will* stumble. That's not a failure. That's life. The trick isn't to avoid failure. It's to bounce back fast with a ritual.

A restart ritual is a pre-decided way to reboot without shame or drama. Examples:

- Reread your anchor habits list.
- Set a mini-goal for the next three days.
- Pick a weekly reset time to review what slipped and decide what to do next.
- Text a friend: "I'm restarting [my habit]. Ask me Friday if I followed through."

Guilt is not a motivator. It's dead weight. It drags you down, making you believe the habit was too hard in the first place.

But a ritual? That's empowering. It gives you a starting line. Again.

SECTION 3: WHAT REALLY MAKES HABITS STICK

CHOOSE FLEXIBILITY

If your habit plan can only survive when everything goes right, it's not a plan; it's a fantasy. Here's what works instead: assume disruption. Build habits that *bend* with your life.

Take exercise. Perhaps your goal is to spend 45 minutes at the gym. Great. However, your backup plan should be something like, "Do 10 pushups before your shower," or, "Take a seven-minute walk after lunch." That's still a win. You're reinforcing the identity of someone who values movement.

Here's a dirty secret of the self-help world: There is no universal habit formula. What works for your friend Zach with his sunrise cold plunges and chia pudding may not necessarily work for you (especially if you hate mornings and don't know what chia is).

Hate running? Don't run. Like playing catch with your kid? Do that. Want to meditate, but sitting still drives you to distraction? Try walking meditation. Or call it "thinking time with fewer screens." Feel free to rebrand it.

The trick is to choose habits you don't dread. You're more likely to repeat something that feels satisfying—or at least not awful.

So instead of adopting someone else's rigid program, design a habit loop you can actually live with:

- The time of day that feels natural
- The format you enjoy
- A duration that's realistic
- An emotional tone that makes you feel *good*, not guilty

This is about sustainability, not punishment.

USE EMOTION AS GLUE

We're told habits are about repetition, but that's only part of the equation. Positive emotion is the glue that makes habits stick.

That's why it matters to *celebrate* small wins. Literally: Smile, say "nice job," or high-five yourself in the mirror. (Yes, it feels ridiculous. Yes, it works.)

The idea isn't to be cheesy; it's to train your brain to associate the habit with feeling successful. And if you feel successful, you're more likely to repeat the behavior. That creates the identity reinforcement loop you're aiming for.

Habit success means doing the thing and feeling good about it.

So, don't wait until you've reached a goal to feel proud. Feel it now. For showing up. For doing anything at all.

One toe-touch still counts.

ADD A HUMAN, DOUBLE YOUR ODDS

Want to double your odds of sticking with a habit? Add another human.

Accountability works—not because it pressures you, but because it *connects* you.

That could mean a workout buddy, a weekly check-in with a friend, or a shared goal with your partner. (Maybe you both want to eat better, or spend less time scrolling at night.) You don't need a coach. You just need someone who knows you're trying and cares if you keep trying.

The point is that we're social animals. When other people are involved, we're more likely to show up because the stakes are higher than merely disappointing ourselves.

So, if you're trying to establish a new habit, don't go it alone. Go with a team. Text a friend, tell your partner, find a group online. Or just say out loud, "This matters to me." (Preferably not in the middle of Costco.)

Good habits aren't built in a vacuum. They're built in the middle of messy lives, shifting schedules, and mood swings that come from not sleeping enough and accidentally reading the comments section.

If your habit system collapses every time your day goes sideways, it's not you; it's the system. Design one that permits you to adapt. Then show up for it—one laughably small action at a time.

KEY TAKEAWAYS FROM CHAPTER 7

1. *Why Flexible Routines Win.* Rigid routines collapse under pressure; flexible ones bend and bounce back. Anchor habits and habit stacking give you a stable foundation without requiring perfection.
2. *Stick With It (Even on Bad Days).* Small steps like the Two-Minute Rule, visual cues, and restart rituals keep you consistent. The win isn't perfection; it's showing up, even when life goes sideways.
3. *What Really Makes Habits Stick.* Habits last when they feel satisfying and supported. Emotion, accountability, and adaptability matter more than willpower or strict discipline.

ACKNOWLEDGMENTS

This chapter was informed by the work of Dr. BJ Fogg, founder of the Stanford Behavior Design Lab; Harvard's

John Beshears, whose research highlights the power of flexibility in habit formation; and James Clear, author of *Atomic Habits*, whose practical guidance on starting small and staying consistent helped shape our approach.

MODERATELY PAINLESS EXERCISES

MPE MAIN: PICK YOUR ANCHOR HABITS AND STACK THEM

We've defined anchor habits and shown how to stack them. Now, let's help you do some picking and stacking.

Step 1: *Identify three habits you already do most days*

List everyday actions that happen without much thought. Aim for things that occur at roughly the same time each day.

Examples: Brush teeth. Pour coffee. Let the dog out. Check email. Start the car.

Step 2: *Choose one micro-habit you want to build*

Choose something that would improve your day if it were to happen regularly. Keep it comically small.

Examples: Write one sentence in a journal. Do five pushups. Take three deep breaths. Text your partner, "I appreciate you." Put one (yes, just one) dish in the dishwasher.

Step 3: *Link the new habit to an existing one*

Use this formula: After I [*anchor habit*], I will [*new habit*]. Examples:

- After I pour my coffee, I'll stretch for 30 seconds.
- After I brush my teeth, I'll write down one thing I'm grateful for.
- After I check my email, I'll close one browser tab I don't need.

Step 4: *Practice it for five days straight*

Don't wait until you "feel ready." Just try it. If you mess up, don't feel guilty. Try again tomorrow.

This isn't about making a massive life change. It's about proving you can add one small win to something you already do. Once you do that, you've just built a real habit, one that bends, not breaks.

MPE MINI: PICK ONE TWO-MINUTE HABIT

Think of one habit you want to build, and then shrink it. Example:

- Want to stretch every morning? New goal: Touch your toes once.
- Want to read more? New goal: Open the book and read one paragraph.

Start with the super simple version for five straight days. Then build from there—if you want. The win is showing up.

CHAPTER 8
REST WITHOUT REGRET

CHAPTER SUMMARY

Needing a break doesn't make you lazy. It makes you human. This chapter reframes rest and leisure as strategic assets, not guilty pleasures. The Moderately Motivated Man discovers how proper downtime improves focus, health, creativity, and relationships. By scheduling rest and making space for hobbies and fun, you not only feel better; you perform better.

SECTION 1: WHY REST IS ESSENTIAL

BURNOUT ISN'T A BADGE

Here's a truth bomb: Saying, "I'm so busy, I got only four hours of sleep" is not a flex. Somewhere along the way, we confused exhaustion with achievement, as if being fried means we're doing life right.

But chronic fatigue is a flashing red warning light on

your dashboard. Ignore it, and your body and brain will get creative showing warning signs: headaches, brain fog, even snapping at the dog for an innocent glance.

The Moderately Motivated Man doesn't wear burnout like a badge. He sees it for what it is: a system failure that needs attention. He understands that rest isn't what you do after the work is done. It's how you do the work well.

PRIORITIZE SLEEP LIKE A PRO

You don't have to track REM cycles or own a $3,000 smart mattress, but you do need to take sleep seriously.

Lack of sleep messes with everything: your memory, focus, patience, and mood—and your judgment as you hit "reply all" on an email that definitely didn't need group involvement.

Skipping sleep might feel like gaining time—until your brain starts charging interest. With compounding fees.

Instead of trying to "catch up" on weekends (spoiler: You can't.), aim for a consistent sleep rhythm. Try the same bedtime, less screen glow, and a wind-down ritual that doesn't involve doomscrolling or finishing off the leftover meatballs at midnight. Give your brain a smooth runway, not a crash landing.

Think of sleep as your daily pit stop. Skip it, and don't be surprised when your wheels come off.

MICRO-BREAKS EQUAL MACRO GAINS

You don't need a week in the Bahamas to feel better (although it probably wouldn't hurt). Sometimes, you only need 90 seconds to breathe.

Short breaks—whether to move or just tune out—

refresh your focus and energy better than that extra cup of coffee. Plus, they don't come with the caffeine crash or the existential dread of realizing it's your third cold brew before noon.

Step outside. Roll your shoulders. Find a tree to gaze at or just stare at a wall. The goal? Interrupt the noise and let your brain reboot.

Pro tip: Schedule your breaks before you need them. Waiting until you're fried is like waiting until your gas tank is on E in the middle of the desert. Don't be that guy.

DO NOTHING (ON PURPOSE)

Here's a wild idea: What if you scheduled a block of time with no goal, no outcome, no purpose except to just be?

Stillness isn't laziness; it's space for your brain to catch its breath. In fact, those quiet, unstructured moments are often where your best ideas show up.

So give yourself permission to do nothing. Sit on a porch. Watch the ceiling fan spin. Let your mind wander without pulling it back on task.

The Moderately Motivated Man knows that sometimes the most productive thing you can do is absolutely nothing.

SECTION 2: THE POWER OF PLAY AND PEOPLE

HOBBIES ARE MORE THAN JUST FUN

Let's get this straight: A hobby is not a cute bonus if you

finish your to-do list. It's a pressure-release valve for your brain and a sparkplug for your mood.

Research backs it up: Hobbies cut stress, ease depression, boost well-being, and give you something more to look forward to than just the weekend.

Hobbies help you manage emotions and prove you're more than merely a walking inbox. They don't need to be impressive. Or turn into a side hustle. You just need something that's yours—and that lights you up.

If you're not sure where to start, think back to what made you happy as a kid. Was it building stuff? Drawing dinosaurs? Hitting a tennis ball off the garage door? There's probably a grown-up version that doesn't involve crayons on the walls.

PUT PLAY ON THE CALENDAR

You wouldn't "just squeeze in" an important meeting, right? So stop treating fun like an afterthought. Put leisure time on your calendar. Literally. Block time for the board game, a hike, your hobby project, or that pickup basketball game where everyone's knees make weird sounds. If it's not scheduled, it's not real.

Play isn't only entertainment; it's a reset button for your brain. It spikes endorphins, lowers anxiety, boosts creativity, and makes you more fun to be around.

And if you want to bond with others? Shared fun is one of the fastest ways to build connection. Laughing together is how real connection happens—no app required.

Fun is not the enemy of productivity. It's part of the plan.

PEOPLE BEFORE PRODUCTIVITY

You can be a machine at clearing your inbox, but without real connection, it's only "productivity" with no point.

Humans are social animals (even the introverts). And strong relationships don't just make life better; they make it healthier. Individuals with strong social connections tend to recover more quickly from stress, illness, and negative news. Those connections are basically emotional Kevlar.

So text your buddy to grab lunch. Call your sibling on a random Tuesday. Sit on the couch and actually talk to your partner instead of watching two separate shows on two separate screens while half-scrolling through TikTok.

Connection doesn't need a big production. It needs presence.

UNPLUG TO RECONNECT

Look, we're not saying screens are evil. (You're reading this on one, possibly.) But too much of a good thing is still too much.

Constant screen time—especially unbroken screen time—fries your brain and steals your focus. It also makes it really hard to feel present, which is kind of the point of life.

You can start small. Declare certain zones device-free: the dinner table, the bedroom, the porch. Or pick a few device-free times: the first 10 minutes after you wake up, meals with family, the hour before bed. Whatever works.

The point isn't perfection; it's awareness. You'll be amazed how much calmer your brain feels when it isn't being yanked every six seconds by a buzz, ping, or breaking news about someone's salad.

Unplug to reconnect with real life.

SECTION 3: MAKE DOWNTIME COUNT

DESIGN YOUR RECHARGE ROUTINE

We all have different "recharge ports." Some guys come alive after a trail run. Others need headphones, a couch, and absolutely no one talking to them.

The key is to know what truly restores you, not what you *think* should work because it looks cool on Instagram. Do you feel better after a walk, a nap, a jam session, or 30 quiet minutes of reorganizing your toolbox in perfect silence?

Create a ritual around that. Make it feel official. Light a candle. Use the "good" coffee mug. Close the door. The point is to signal to your brain, "Hey, this is the good stuff. We're recharging now."

BUILD IN BREAKS (BEFORE YOU BREAK DOWN)

The Moderately Motivated Man doesn't sprint through the day until he collapses on the couch like a broken robot. He knows that downtime works best when it's built in, not postponed until it's too late.

Try spacing your breaks throughout the day on purpose. A five-minute breather every hour. An authentic lunch away from your screen. A walk between work and evening responsibilities. These are reset buttons that keep your system running smoothly.

It's not laziness; it's maintenance, like changing your oil before your car engine seizes.

And if you're the kind of guy who always says, "I'll relax

after this next thing..." try this: Assume there's always a next thing. Schedule the break anyway.

EMBRACE DOWNTIME, DROP THE GUILT

What's one of the sneakier reasons we skip rest? It feels indulgent, especially if someone else is working while we're not.

But guilt is not a productivity tool; it's a joy thief. Truthfully, your downtime might be the most responsible thing you do all day. It makes you a better partner, parent, coworker, and person who doesn't lose his mind when the Wi-Fi goes out.

Make downtime visible. Discuss it as you would a gym session or a Monday morning meeting. Normalize rest in your own household and among your friends. Be the guy who says, "I can't this afternoon. I'm unplugging for an hour." Watch how others start to follow suit.

Downtime deserves its place in the spotlight. Don't stash it away like a guilty secret.

DEFINE REST YOUR WAY

Here's a trap: Thinking rest only "counts" if it looks a certain way. Yoga mat. Candle. Monastery. Wrong.

Rest is what restores you. That could be building a birdhouse, hitting golf balls at the range, or organizing your garage while listening to 90s hip hop. It could be sitting in a diner with a buddy, not talking much, but still filling your tank.

Don't get caught chasing someone else's version of restoration. Define your own.

And remember: What counts is how you *feel*, not how it looks to others.

The world is full of advice about how to grind harder, sleep less, and squeeze more out of every waking moment. That advice often comes from people who look permanently stressed and secretly take afternoon naps.

But the best version of you isn't the one who never stops. It's the one who knows when to recharge—and actually does.

KEY TAKEAWAYS FROM CHAPTER 8

1. *Why Rest Is Essential.* Rest isn't laziness; it's fuel. Sleep, breaks, and even doing nothing on purpose restore your focus, mood, and energy so you can show up better in every part of life.
2. *The Power of Play and People.* Hobbies, fun, and connection aren't extras; they're essentials. Play resets your brain, and meaningful relationships build resilience and joy.
3. *Make Downtime Count.* Breaks work best when they're built in, visible, and guilt-free. Define what rest means for you, and protect it as fiercely as you protect your work.

ACKNOWLEDGMENTS

Portions of this chapter were informed by Alex Soojung-Kim Pang's article "How Resting More Can Boost Your Productivity" (Greater Good Science Center), which explores the science behind rest as a performance enhancer. Insights into the upside of hobbies were adapted from

"Health Benefits of Hobbies" by Venkat S.R. on WebMD, and themes about digital boundaries were supported by Dr. H. Kelley Riley's piece, "The Power of Unplugging," on SummaCare.com.

MODERATELY PAINLESS EXERCISES

MPE MAIN: DESIGN YOUR PERSONAL RECHARGE MENU

You know how restaurants have a menu of go-to options? You need one for recharging. Not everything will work every day, but when you're wiped, it helps to have ideas ready so your brain doesn't have to improvise.

Step 1: *List Three Quick Recharge Moves*

These are things that take 10 minutes or less. Think:

- A walk around the block
- Stretching to your favorite song
- Playing fetch with your dog ... or your kid

Step 2: *Add Three Medium Recharge Moves*

These take a bit more time (10–30 minutes). Think:

- Reading something non-work-related
- Shooting hoops
- Noodling on your guitar

Step 3: *Add Three Deep Recharge Moves*

These are your real resets, the ones you schedule when you're running low. Think:

- Hitting a trail, a park, or your own backyard with zero agenda
- A hobby night
- A weekend catch-up with a good friend

Post the list somewhere visible, like on your desk, in your notes app, or even on the fridge. The next time you feel exhausted, don't push through. Pick from your menu, and hit reset like a pro.

MPE MINI: PLAN A "POINTLESS" BREAK

This week, schedule 20 minutes to do something purely enjoyable—with no agenda, productivity angle, or multitasking allowed:

- Read a comic book.
- Toss a ball against the garage.
- Stare at a tree.
- Build something, nap, doodle, or daydream.

Whatever you choose, do it just because it feels good. You're not "wasting time"; you're restoring it. Your brain will thank you. So will everyone who deals with you afterward.

CHAPTER 9
BECOME YOUR BEST SELF

CHAPTER SUMMARY

This chapter offers simple ways to stay grounded and present in daily life, helping you reduce stress and accomplish more without undue strain. It highlights how the way you use your time reflects what you value. It also shows how small, manageable choices shape who you are becoming. By learning to keep your attention where it matters, you can become a better version of yourself, without burning out or adding unnecessary pressure. Because success doesn't have to be stressful.

BEFORE WE BEGIN: WHY THIS CHAPTER MATTERS

You've navigated the heart of this book and covered a lot of ground. In earlier chapters, we've already explored:

- Prioritizing what matters (Chapter 2)

- Deep focus and managing distractions (Chapter 3)
- Breaks and boundaries (Chapter 4)
- Procrastination and starting small (Chapter 5)
- Saying no and managing commitments (Chapter 6)
- Habit-building with flexibility (Chapter 7)
- Rest, play, and connection (Chapter 8)

This chapter isn't about rehashing all of that. This is a chance to weave the threads together.

Time management isn't just about tactics. It's also about who you become through the small, repeated choices you make. This chapter invites you to reflect on that journey.

It's a capstone. A zoom-out moment. A chance to take stock of how far you've come—not in terms of tasks completed, but in how you think about your time, your energy, and your direction.

So if this chapter feels a little more reflective, that's on purpose. We're closing the loop without pep talks or pressure—just some calm, honest encouragement to keep going and keep becoming the man you're trying to be.

SECTION 1: STAY GROUNDED IN THE MOMENT

ATTENTION IS WHERE LIFE HAPPENS

Let's be honest: Most of us live about five minutes ahead of ourselves.

You're replying to emails while half-listening to your

partner, thinking about dinner during meetings, or running tomorrow's to-do list while supposedly playing LEGO with your kid. Your body is here, but your attention is lost on a mental hamster wheel.

The goal here isn't enlightenment or perfect calm. It's simply to be present. The ability to show up fully where you are, instead of scattering yourself across tabs, texts, and tomorrow.

Time passes whether you like it or not. But attention? That's where life actually happens.

Where you put your attention determines what you experience, what you remember, and who you become. You can go through an entire day and not feel like you were really there because your attention was elsewhere the whole time.

Mental energy drains quickly when scattered in a dozen directions. But when you focus it carefully—on a task, person, or moment—you accomplish more, feel grounded, and ironically, reclaim time by not constantly rebooting your brain.

Let's be honest. Being present is hard—really hard, actually, in our fast-paced world. So we often need some help to stay in the moment and make the most of our time.

MICRO-HABITS TO REFOCUS

You don't need a yoga mat to refocus. You merely need 30 seconds and a breath.

- Try this: Inhale slowly. Hold it. Exhale even slower. Feel your shoulders drop.
- Or this: Look around. Name three things you

see, two things you hear, and one thing you can
touch. Boom—you're back.
- Or: Pause for 30 seconds and notice you're alive.
Sense your breath, your body, your feet on the
floor. Your mind will wander. Let it. Then come
back to whatever you were doing.

These micro-resets can be tucked into any busy day, even between meetings or before a tough conversation. They come in handy after your kid spills applesauce on your keyboard. They're tiny anchors to the now. And in a world of constant buzz, that's powerful stuff.

AVOID THE DISTRACTION SPIRAL

You're not a failure because your brain drifts. That's what brains do, especially human ones.

The trick isn't to shame yourself when you've been scrolling Reddit for 20 minutes. It's to notice it and gently return.

That ability to bring yourself back without judgment is powerful. The Moderately Motivated Man doesn't aim for flawless concentration. He aims for awareness and then makes the best next choice.

Some days, your brain is oatmeal. You forget the day, pour coffee in your cereal, and waste 30 minutes fighting with a printer that's not even plugged in.

Progress isn't about perfect days; it's about sticking with the process even on the weird ones. Self-compassion keeps you going when only grit would make you quit. On off-days, grace goes further than grind.

SECTION 2: YOUR TIME REFLECTS WHO YOU ARE

ACTIONS SPEAK LOUDER THAN INTENTIONS

Actions don't lie. You might say family matters, but if work consumes every extra hour, what is that saying? You say you want to write a book, but if Netflix wins every night... well, you see the point.

None of this is meant to guilt you. It's intended to empower you. Because once you realize your time is a mirror of your values, you can make small shifts that start reflecting the man you want to be, not just the man you default to when life gets noisy.

If most of your time goes to reacting to requests, notifications, and obligations, then it's no wonder you feel like a pinball. But when you start claiming a little space each day for what matters to you, that's identity work. You can do it one time block at a time.

This doesn't mean becoming hyper-efficient. It means making space—even 15 minutes—for the things that nourish your real goals: connecting with your kids, going for a walk, or reading something that sharpens your thinking. These are the moments that shift your trajectory.

SMALL DECISIONS ADD UP

Think of your time like compound interest. Each little intentional choice adds up, especially when repeated:

- Saying no to that extra meeting.
- Taking five minutes to plan your day.

- Spending 10 minutes journaling or reflecting before bed.
- Calling your dad on the way home instead of counting out-of-state license plates.

These choices are small, but they build. Then they begin to align your time with your values, which creates a virtuous circle.

KEEP YOUR SCHEDULE REAL

You don't need to run your life like a Fortune 500 CEO. You just need a schedule that fits your rhythms.

- Are you sharper in the morning? Use that window for deep work, not email roulette.
- Do you crash after lunch? Schedule admin stuff or low-energy tasks.
- Need more space on Wednesdays because life gets nuts? Build that in.

The Moderately Motivated Man doesn't try to conquer time. He flows with it. He listens to his own rhythms. He also adjusts because no two days are exactly alike. That's not failure. That's flexibility.

SECTION 3: LIVE LIFE ON PURPOSE

YOUR TIME IS A VOTE—CAST IT WISELY

This chapter isn't here to ask you to reinvent yourself. It's here to ask: Based on how you're spending your time, are you already becoming the guy you want to be—or drifting into someone else's idea of success?

You don't need to overhaul your life. You only need to live a little more deliberately. In this section, we connect the dots: how daily choices shape identity, how your time signals your values to others, and how steady action (not epic ambition) changes the game.

Every day, you cast votes. Not on a ballot, but with your attention, calendar, and energy.

Each action is a vote for what matters. Over time, those actions mold your identity—not in one dramatic moment, but in hundreds of little choices: whether you hit snooze or stretch, whether you scroll or listen, whether you cancel or show up.

Seeing time as a vote reveals you're not just reacting; you're building. Ask yourself: What kind of man do I want to become? Then check your calendar. Is the reality matching the vision?

Even if the answer is no, that's okay. Now you've got data. Adjust. Cast your votes differently tomorrow.

DROP THE PERFECT-MAN MYTH

Let's get honest about perfection. A lot of guys get stuck trying to become the "ideal man" version of themselves—the one who wakes up at 5 a.m., crushes work, remembers birthdays, makes smart investments, and never forgets to floss.

Spoiler: The perfect guy doesn't exist. Or if he does, you wouldn't want to hang out with him. He's probably insufferable. (Which would prove he isn't perfect!)

Real progress looks messier. It's built on effort, not image. It's saying, "I'm trying" and meaning it. So instead of chasing some imaginary optimized version of yourself, just aim for "a little better than last week."

And if today's better? Great. If it's not? Reset tomorrow.

CLOSE THE GAP, GRADUALLY

There's always a gap between your ideal self and the person you currently are. What matters is noticing that gap and then closing it, a little at a time.

This doesn't mean revamping your life all at once. It means being honest about what's working, what's not, and where you're phoning it in, and then adjusting with small tweaks or course corrections.

You're not a robot. You're a guy navigating real life with real distractions and real responsibilities. Owning your time is how you close that gap—not to impress anyone, but because it's the best way to live on your own terms.

When you do that, you don't merely "manage" time. You lead it.

The Moderately Motivated Man doesn't need to announce he's evolving. He quietly does the work. Not flashy. Not flawless. But steady.

This chapter offers perspective. You now have tools to stay present, filter out noise, align your time with your values, and build a calendar that reflects who you truly want to be.

That doesn't happen in a weekend. It occurs in the choices you make today and again tomorrow.

Small steps lead to a big impact. Reading this book was a significant step. You've got this.

KEY TAKEAWAYS FROM CHAPTER 9

1. *Stay Grounded in the Moment.* Attention is where life actually happens. Small resets—like breathing breaks or brief pauses—help you stay present and avoid scattering your energy across distractions.
2. *Your Time Reflects Who You Are.* The way you spend your hours is a mirror of your values. Even small, consistent choices cast votes for the kind of man you want to become.
3. *Live Life On Purpose.* You don't need a flawless plan or a perfect version of yourself. Progress comes from steady, intentional actions that bring clarity, balance, and a stronger sense of direction.

ACKNOWLEDGMENTS

This chapter drew inspiration from Conrad Ruiz's article "Men Should Manage Their Time Better and Here Are 3 Reasons Why" (The Man Effect), which emphasized time as a form of leadership and identity, and from Barnabas Payam's "Effect of Time Management on Men" (Vocal.Media), which reinforced the connection between time use, self-care, and relational growth.

MODERATELY PAINLESS EXERCISES

MPE MAIN: THE "IDENTITY BLOCK" BUILDER

The guy you're aiming to be probably isn't that far off. Let's keep building him. In this exercise, you can take 30 minutes to act like the man you're trying to become.

Step 1: *Pick Your Identity Word*

Think about the kind of guy you're aiming to be more of. (*We talked about this in Chapter 1.*) Not Perfect Man™—just a bit more intentional, grounded, or energized. Choose one identity to focus on this week. Examples:

- "Present Dad"
- "Healthy Guy"
- "Strategic Thinker"
- "Family-First Son"

Don't overthink it. Pick the version of you that could use a little reinforcement right now.

Step 2: *Block It In*

Open your calendar or planner and find one 30-minute slot in the next seven days. Label that time with the identity you picked. For example:

- Wednesday 7:30 a.m.—Healthy Guy: Walk & stretch
- Friday 12:30 p.m.—Strategic Thinker: Sketch out next week's big priorities
- Sunday 4:00 p.m.—Family-First Son: Actually call Mom this time

Treat this like an appointment, because it is. It's a meeting with Future You.

Step 3: *Show Up and Do the Thing*

When that time arrives, honor the block. Be present. No rescheduling. No half-credit. Do the thing, and notice how it feels to act in alignment with who you want to be.
Forget perfect. Just cast your vote.

Bonus: *Repeat Weekly*

Once a week, book one more "identity block." Build the habit of turning your intentions into actions. Keep it light. Keep it honest. Keep moving in the direction that feels like yours.

MPE MINI: YOUR "FUTURE YOU" TIME CHECK

Take 10 minutes to do a no-pressure calendar review. Grab your phone or planner, and scroll through your past week. Ask yourself the following:

- What do I say is important ... but never makes the calendar?
- What's getting too much time for the payoff it brings?
- Where can I replace one "meh" task with something more meaningful?

Pick one shift to make next week. Only one. Not a life overhaul—just one vote for the man you're becoming. Then keep casting votes.

CHAPTER 10
USE TOOLS THAT WORK

CHAPTER SUMMARY

Time management tools are like gym memberships: Getting one won't change your life, but using it the right way might. This chapter rounds up a set of beginner-friendly digital tools that can help you track time, plan your day, manage tasks, and stay focused, without feeling like you've enrolled in a productivity boot camp. These are practical apps and systems to help a Moderately Motivated Man get a little more done (and feel a little less scattered doing it).

THE THREE TOOL CATEGORIES THAT MATTER

There are a million productivity tools out there, which is precisely the problem. If you've ever Googled "best time management apps," you probably got buried in a landslide of listicles and acronyms. Here's a more straightforward approach:

Let's break time management tools into three broad categories:

1. Planning & Scheduling Tools:

These help you map out your day or week. Think of them like the modern version of a paper calendar or a whiteboard—only with alarms and cloud syncing.

2. Task Management Tools:

These tools help you capture, prioritize, and finish your to-dos, so your brain isn't juggling tasks during your kid's soccer game.

3. Focus & Attention Tools:

These help reduce distractions and increase your chances of doing one thing at a time, instead of toggling between six browser tabs, two Slack messages, and an unfinished email.

That's it. Everything useful lives in one (or more) of these buckets. Now let's look at the best of the bunch.

SECTION NO. 1: PLANNING & SCHEDULING TOOLS—PUT IT ON THE CALENDAR

GOOGLE CALENDAR (FREE)

Why it works: You probably already have it, and that's the point. No learning curve, no software to install. Google

Calendar is a simple, visual way to see your time, not just think about it.

How to use it like a grown-up:

- Create a dedicated calendar for "Me Time"—workouts, reading, or even nothing at all.
- Time-block tasks. Don't merely *hope* you'll get to it. Put "Call accountant" at 4:30 p.m. You'll be shocked how much more real it feels.
- Set alerts 10 minutes before each event. That alone can rescue you from the time vortex of your inbox.

Bonus Tip: Color-code your calendar: blue for work, green for personal, and red for must-do tasks. Soon, your calendar will reveal your true priorities.

MOTION (PAID; FREE TRIAL)

Why it's different: Motion blends a calendar with a task manager and automatically reshuffles your to-dos when life derails your day. It's like a digital assistant who knows life gets messy.

Best for: Guys who overestimate what they can do in one day and underestimate how long things take. (So, most of us.)

Watch Out For: Some users find it takes a little getting used to. If you prefer more manual control, it might feel like the app's running the show instead of you.

SECTION NO. 2: TASK MANAGEMENT TOOLS—FROM BRAIN DUMP TO DONE

TODOIST (FREE + PAID TIERS)

Why it works: Todoist is essentially the digital version of writing things down and crossing them off—except it's way less likely to get thrown out with the pizza box.

Key features for normal humans:

- Easy keyboard shortcuts and quick-add tasks
- Natural language input (type "Call dentist Tuesday at 10 a.m."; it'll figure it out)
- Daily reminders, recurring tasks, priority tags

How to keep it simple:

- Start with a single "Today" list.
- Don't worry about categories, karma points, or productivity streaks.
- Build the habit: Open it each morning, and close it with one win.

TRELLO (FREE + PAID TIERS)

Why people love it: It's visual. Trello turns tasks into cards and projects into boards you can shuffle at will. Think digital sticky notes you can move around as life shifts.

Great for:

- Managing ongoing projects (like planning a vacation or organizing the garage)

- Tracking progress (To Do → Doing → Done boards are oddly satisfying)
- Collaborating with your spouse or team without endless texts

MMM tip: Trello's flexibility can be a trap. Don't try to build a second brain. Use it to track the handful of things you're actually trying to finish this week.

SECTION NO. 3: FOCUS & ATTENTION TOOLS—GUARDRAILS FOR YOUR BRAIN

POMODORO TIMER APPS (LIKE FOCUS KEEPER, FOREST)

Why they work: The Pomodoro Method is straightforward. You work for 25 minutes, then take a five-minute break. Repeat. The timers keep you honest.

Best for:

- Starting a task you've been avoiding
- Staying engaged without feeling chained to your desk
- Building up your attention span like a muscle

Tip: Try one Pomodoro a day on an important-but-annoying task. You might be amazed at what 25 focused minutes can do.

RESCUETIME (FREE + PAID TIERS)

What it does: Tracks how you actually spend time on your devices, not how you *wish* you did.

Why it matters: You can't fix what you can't see. RescueTime shines a light on your actual time spend: emails, Slack, social media, and news included. It's all there.

For beginners:

- Don't get obsessed with the numbers. Use the insights to tweak one habit, not overhaul your whole life.
- Set one daily goal—something like, "Less than 30 minutes of social media."

Surprising perk: RescueTime's end-of-week summary email can be weirdly motivating. Like a productivity report card without a teacher conference required.

EXTRA TOOLS NO. 1: NOTETAKING & DIGITAL BRAIN TOOLS (OPTIONAL, BUT HANDY)

These aren't required, but if you often feel like your thoughts are scattered across sticky notes, text threads, and the back of receipts, a solid notetaking tool might help you reclaim your brain space.

NOTION (FREE + PAID TIERS)

Why people swear by it: It's like LEGO for productivity. You can build dashboards, checklists, databases, habit trackers—whatever suits your style.

For the Moderately Motivated Man: Stick with the basics. Use it to do the following:

- Jot down ideas.
- Create a weekly review template.
- Keep a simple reading list or "watch later" queue.

Word of warning: Notion can turn into a second job if you try to master every feature. Keep it low-lift.

EVERNOTE (FREE + PAID TIERS)

Why it's still around: It's simple, familiar, and great for dumping thoughts into one searchable place.
Best features:

- Web clipper (save articles to read later, not now-now-now)
- Voice notes (if you think best while pacing)
- Tagging, filing and letting future-you rediscover it

EXTRA TOOLS NO. 2: TOOLS THAT ARE OVERKILL (FOR NOW)

Sure, there are tons of powerful tools out there, but that doesn't mean they're right for you.

Here's a shortlist of ones you probably don't need now:

- Jira, Asana, ClickUp, and Coda—These are powerful project management tools made for teams. If you're flying solo, they'll feel like renting a bulldozer to dig a tomato garden.
- Slack, Miro, GitHub—These are great for

companies but less helpful for individuals trying to remember to call the plumber.
- Time trackers with too much detail—If you're spending more time tracking your time than doing anything ... well, you see the problem.

WRAPPING UP THE TOOLBOX

You're not seeking the perfect system. You need a few tools you'll actually use. (And if you prefer good ol' pen and paper? Fantastic.)

Pick one place to plan your week, one place to track your tasks, and one tool to help you focus. That's it.

If something stops working, replace it. No guilt, no ceremony.

This chapter isn't about mastering apps; it's about finding supports that fit your life. The right tools make it easier to follow through on what matters.

Start small. Adjust as needed. Keep your time feeling like it belongs to you.

KEY TAKEAWAYS FROM CHAPTER 10

1. *Planning & Scheduling Tools.* Your calendar isn't just a reminder system; it's a mirror of your priorities. Use simple planning tools to time-block what matters (such as work, family, or rest), so it actually happens.
2. *Task Management Tools.* Your brain isn't built to juggle 50 open loops. Offload your to-dos into a simple task manager, so you can spend your effort doing instead of remembering.

3. *Focus & Attention Tools.* Attention is finite. Use timers, tracking apps, or even a one-tab setup to reduce distractions and make it easier to finish what you start.

ACKNOWLEDGMENTS

This chapter benefited from insights in "15 Best Time Management Tools" by Scarlett Adams (The Knowledge Academy), "18 Essential Productivity Tools Recommended by Tech Experts" (Forbes Technology Council), and Ryan Zofay's "Top 10 Best Life-Changing Time Management Tools." These sources helped identify tools that are widely used and helpful for beginners, reinforcing the chapter's goal of recommending practical, not over-engineered, solutions.

MODERATELY PAINLESS EXERCISES

MPE MAIN: THE TOOL SAMPLER WEEK

Here's your challenge: Run a one-week experiment to find your starter kit.

Step 1: *Pick one tool from each category*

- Planning: Google Calendar or Motion
- Task Management: Todoist or Trello
- Focus: Focus Keeper or RescueTime

Step 2: *Use them for one week, lightly*

- Add 3–5 events to your calendar
- Track 3–5 tasks for the week
- Try 2–3 focus sessions using your focus tool

Step 3: *At the end of the week, ask yourself:*

- Which tool did I enjoy using most?
- Which one actually helped me?
- Which one felt like homework?

That's your signal. Build around what works. Leave the rest. You're not running an HR department; you're just trying to stay on top of life.

MPE MINI: JUST TRY THIS: THE 5-MINUTE TOOL TEST

Choose any time management tool from this chapter: app, planner, timer, whatever.

Spend five minutes using it on something tangible:

- Add a task to a to-do list.
- Schedule one thing in your calendar.
- Start a 25-minute focus timer.

Then ask yourself: Did it make anything easier?

If yes, keep going. If no, no guilt—just try again another time, or simply move on. Not every tool earns a second date.

CONCLUSION

TIME WELL SPENT

If you made it this far in *The Moderately Motivated Man's Guide to Time Management*, two things are true:

- You care about your time.
- You didn't need a life coach in a headset to get here.

That's no small thing.

Time management isn't about having perfectly managed calendars or inboxes with zero emails. It's not about getting "everything done." It's about doing *the right things*, and doing them in a way that doesn't suck the life out of you.

This book has shown you what that looks like in the real world.

You've faced the fact that time is limited and realized that's a gift, not a sentence. Along the way, you've learned that choosing what matters beats chasing what's urgent, multitasking is a myth, and rest is maintenance, not reward.

You've wrestled with procrastination and perfectionism, built habits that bend instead of break, and—most important—made space for the people you love, and for the man you're quietly becoming.

In short: You've done the work.

Not all of it. Not perfectly. Not forever. You've done enough to move the needle, prove you're not stuck, and remember that change isn't about becoming someone else. It's about becoming more of your best self.

If this book gave you even one tool you'll keep, one mindset shift that stuck, or one laugh that eased the process, then it has already paid off. But odds are, you've picked up a lot more than that.

And the best part? The refresher courses are right here, at your fingertips.

SO WHAT'S NEXT

Keep going. Keep testing. Keep blocking off 30 minutes to live with purpose. Say yes to what matters and no to what drains you.

With our 10 chapters, we gave you 10 clear ways to declutter your days and win back your time. Together, they form a toolkit you can return to whenever you need.

Revisit a chapter when you feel lost. Share it with someone else who might need it. Try a new tool. Ditch an old one. Adjust.

You don't need to hustle harder, optimize everything, or get a motivational quote tattooed on your forearm.

CONCLUSION

Just keep showing up with a little more clarity, a little more control, and a little more confidence that your time—messy, limited, real-life time—is truly valuable. Thanks for spending some of it here.

You've got the tools. You've got the time. Make sure it's well spent.

ABOUT THE AUTHOR

Rick Resnick is a former newspaper writer, magazine publisher, and longtime media executive who spent decades helping his companies sell hundreds of millions in advertising dollars—often by crafting custom campaigns that connected brands with consumers. His byline appeared in sponsored features across *Fortune, Time, Money, People,* and *Sports Illustrated.*

As a leader of large marketing teams (and as a husband and father), Rick learned time management the hard way—between meetings, deadlines, and inbox avalanches. He practiced what he now preaches: blocking "thinking time" on his calendar, protecting deep work, and occasionally booking conference rooms just to escape phone calls, emails, and drive-by interruptions.

His first book, *The New Husband's Survival Guide*, offered laugh-out-loud advice for men trying to coexist peacefully with women. Now he's tackling productivity with *The Moderately Motivated Man's Guide to Time Management*—the first in a self-help series for guys who want to get better at life without trying too hard.

When he's not writing, Rick plays tennis and golf, obsessively supports Arsenal FC, and sings lead in a rock cover band based in Pike County, PA. He still checks email too often, but he's working on it.

THANK YOU FOR READING

BEFORE YOU GO

You made it to the last page. Now you've got practical ways to win back your time—without joining the 5 a.m. "rise-and-grind" club.

One small favor: If this book helped you, a short review on your favorite book site can help other Moderately Motivated Men discover it. A few quick sentences mean more than you'd think.

For updates on future books, you can join the MMM mailing list: signup.ModeratelyMotivatedMan.com

And if you know someone who's always "too busy" for his own good, consider telling him about this book.

With appreciation—Rick Resnick

contact.ModeratelyMotivatedMan.com

www.ingramcontent.com/pod-product-compliance
Lightning Source LLC
LaVergne TN
LVHW041611070526
838199LV00052B/3085